Praises for the Author

"Barbara Gabogrecan is an extremely motivated and multi-talented individual whose generous spirit appears boundless. Her no-nonsense approach to fielding another curved ball in her game of life or death, is truly inspirational." **Jane Woods; Proof The Proof**

"I was totally amazed by the way in which Barbara coped throughout the ordeal of the stroke, the shock of discovering that she couldn't read and the operation to remove a brain tumour. This is an inspirational journey to recovery as Barbara was able to empathise with and encourage others whilst retaining an indomitable attitude and a sense of humour." **Anne Morton; Lifestyle Video Productions**

"Barbara has a great gift which takes you on an inspiring journey. Personal insights and stories about her life, as well as her journey of recovery, make this book a 'must read', not only for stroke survivors, but for everyone!" **Robyn O'Connell; Celebrant & Author**

"I have always admired your perseverance and optimism whenever you get a new idea into your head. I know your bravery and insights will encourage others." **Lyn Roy**

Also by the Author

E-Book Marketing and Selling (e-book)
Business Solutions @ Work (e-book)
How Do You Eat an Elephant? (e-book)
Are You Ready to Start a Business? (e-book)
Fast Track Your Marketing (e-book)
Home Based Business Ideas (e-book)
How to Run a Business from Your Kitchen Table (print)

Thank God I Had a *Stroke*

A Stroke and Brain Tumour
Survivor's Journey of Recovery

BARBARA GABOGRECAN

BALBOA
PRESS

A DIVISION OF HAY HOUSE

Balboa Press books may be ordered through booksellers or by contacting:

Balboa Press
A Division of Hay House
1663 Liberty Drive
Bloomington, IN 47403
www.balboapress.com.au
1-(877) 407-4847

ISBN: 978-1-4525-0980-8 (sc)
ISBN: 978-1-4525-0981-5 (e)

Printed in the United States of America

Balboa Press rev. date: 04/15/2013

In memory of my mother, Esma Frances Deece.
She gave me the courage to be me.

When you see something, you will forget it. When you hear something, you will remember it. But not until you do something will you understand it.

-Anonymous

CONTENTS

FOREWORD

I met Barbara on the neurology ward in June 2011 at the time of her stroke. I was impressed with how quickly she adjusted to her situation. One of the first questions she asked me was, "Will I be able to read again?"

What followed was a journey of discovery as Barbara examined, assessed, and discovered what she did and didn't have. The human being in time can conquer and compensate for lost ability and indeed, this is what she has taught me.

A sudden impairment of brain function can be incapacitating, especially if it affects your communication skills. It is especially traumatic if you depend on those skills for your living.

To have a deep-seated brain tumour, discovered incidentally at the time of a stroke, is a lot for any person to digest.

On June 10, 2011, Barbara underwent a complex operation to remove her brain tumour, and through motivation and perseverance, she made a speedy recovery. Looking after Barbara in hospital, I noticed how she cared and involved herself with those around her. No doubt, this was a small reflection of her lifetime spent caring for others.

I am sure her life experience (as told in this book) will inspire those who read it. There are lessons learned for those of us in health care on perspectives through the eyes of the patient. There are lessons for all of us on how we can successfully meet significant challenges in life.

Congratulations, Barbara on achieving this publication within barely a year of such major life events. I am sure you will charge on with life!

Mr. Arul Bala, MBBS (Hons.), FRACS (N. Surg.)

PREFACE

I have always congratulated myself on my strength of character, my determination, and my ability to take on a number of tasks with vigour and passion.

I have also had a strong desire to help others by sharing my experiences and skills with them. To watch others make changes to their lives so that their confidence and self-assurance grows because of my support gives me a sense of achievement and a great deal of pleasure and satisfaction.

Even though I think I have coped with many difficult problems in my life, they paled into insignificance when compared to the life threatening double whammy I experienced by having to mentally and physically cope with both a stroke and a brain tumour at the same time.

As I dealt with each stage of my illness, I wanted to share my journey with others who might be suffering from similar illnesses. I am sure that my goal-oriented approach to my illness helped with my recovery. By sharing my journey, I hope that others might also find solace and inspiration during their time of suffering.

In my case, the love and support of my husband Pete was a major factor in the speed of my recovery. Therefore, I also wanted to let the loved ones caring for those suffering understand what they are going through and just how critical their support is for a final, triumphant recovery.

In the process of wanting to help the sufferers and their caregivers, I have told my story as I really *felt* it. However, I did not expect the medical team to find something of value in this narrative. I was therefore surprised when Mr. Bala, my surgeon, said, "From a medical perspective, it was valuable seeing your honest insight of the entire hospital experience." Nurses and other professionals from my medical support team also indicated that they were keen to read my story. It would help them better understand exactly how patients felt about the treatment and help they got when in hospital, and they could therefore better assist in the care of these patients.

This story is not simply a chronology or a factual medical interpretation. I wrote it around my own emotional, and at times frightening, experiences. I designed it to inspire and enthuse readers to enable those suffering to cope with their illness and to see the light at the end of the tunnel.

INTRODUCTION

Peter O'Connor

B arbara had quite a unique early life that was different from what most children in Australia experienced. It was definitely foreign to children such as me, who were born and grew up in the city. She was brought up in the bush where her dad managed sheep properties and broke in horses. Her entire network consisted of the family: her mum, dad, and two younger brothers (Jimmy and Fred). Barbara and Jimmy completed their primary schooling by correspondence and learnt to be self-sufficient, confident, determined, and resourceful.

This lifestyle meant that Barbara did miss out on a number of social skills, such as how to respond and react with her peers, but her unusual upbringing helped shape her into the strong and resilient person she is today.

There is no doubt in my mind that Barbara's early life gave her both the strength and courage to cope with having a stroke and brain tumour. Her incredible journey through trauma, acceptance, and eventually recovery is a testament to her strength of character that developed in those early years.

As Barbara matured, another trait that became obvious was her desire to care for and share information with others. She treated her career of teaching art more like a vocation than a job. She had a fierce determination to share her knowledge and experience with her young students and took great delight in watching students hone their creative skills, enabling them to achieve far beyond their own expectations.

I remember one occasion when she and three senior students spent a weekend outdoors painting a complex landscape. Barbara and one of her students sold their paintings to a gallery, and Barbara was ecstatic to learn that the student sold his for double what she received!

Barbara carried this enthusiasm into the next stage of her life when she developed a successful art business and began to mentor other start-up business operators. She decided to develop Home Based Business Australia to give herself a platform from which she could share information and enthuse and motivate her colleagues as they developed their own businesses. Barbara encouraged me to help her build a number of websites and blogs to further assist the home-business sector. Her three main sites were listed on page one of Google, which was no mean feat for someone who was a self-confessed "dummy" when it came to technology.

Barbara then wrote a number of business self-help books and became a renowned key speaker both in Australia and overseas. She also organised a number of prestigious events, including awards for small business. The awards attracted major sponsors as well as state government departments to help run them throughout Australia.

All of Barbara's efforts were aimed at helping micro and home based businesses. It did not take long for her to became known as the "home-business guru," and a number of government departments (federal, state, and local) invited her to sit on various committees and advise them on the needs of the sector.

I feel that writing this book was simply another platform for Barbara to share her experiences for the benefit of others. Instead of targeting business operators, her story is now aimed at helping those going through the same traumas as she did or for loved ones trying to cope with those who are suffering. It therefore surprised both her and me when a number of medical professionals (from nurses to doctors) said they felt it was also important for them to understand how the patient felt and coped with the trauma of a serious illness. Apparently, these professionals were also keen to read her book.

Barbara has always thrived on setting goals, as they provide her with challenges that give a real boost to her ego and build her confidence, allowing her to move forward with gusto and passion. Writing this book was a major goal that she enthusiastically strove to fulfil, at a time when she desperately needed a "trigger" to boost her morale. I am sure that Barbara did not fully realise just how difficult it was going to be. I witnessed her struggle with her handicap during the writing of this book, and I was just so pleased that I was there and able to help her to the degree that I did.

It wasn't just me who encouraged, supported, and loved her during her time of trauma and recovery. Her mum and eldest son, Mark, who lives with us, were always there for her too. Her two younger brothers, Jimmy and Fred, lived in other states, and she did not get to see them very often. During her illness, Jimmy rang regularly to check on how she was coping and Fred actually made the trip from interstate to the hospital to see her for the first time in nearly ten years. I know that she was really chuffed by this, as she missed Fred a great deal.

Barbara has two sons: Mark and Billy. Mark has experienced many problems throughout his life of forty-five years, from the time of his birth when Barbara clinically died for three minutes to now as he struggles to lose excess weight. Mark has never married and has become an "uncle figure" to the many children of his friends.

Her younger son, Billy, is in the army, and Barbara seldom sees him with his overseas postings and constant movement from one state to another. As a youngster, he was very involved with theatre and dance, where he won many competitions and scholarships. When he began to grow into a sturdy, robust teenager, he stopped it all and joined the army, where he trained to be a signalman. I know Barbara would have loved him to do ballroom dancing or retain an interest in theatre, but that was not to be.

I am Barbara's second husband, and she is my second wife; we are true soul mates. At five-foot, nine, I am a little taller than Barbara and have had a shock of white hair (now thinning) since my midtwenties. I used to drive a taxi part time and my nickname was "The Silver Fox." Barbara has always said my hair made me look sophisticated and stylish; I'm not so sure about that!

As a former teacher, Barbara cannot believe that I failed every subject in my matriculation year, including English, for which I was awarded zero marks. Barbara tells me that this result was a perfect example of why individual schools and their teachers should not mark the papers of their own students. This procedure was eventually dropped and all students sat the exams externally and could only be identified by numbers.

I know that one of the reasons why I did so poorly at school was because I devoted my life at that time to rowing and football. I now pay the penalty with a chronic back condition and worn-out knees.

My first marriage was a disaster. The only good things to come out of it were the two daughters that we had. One now lives in Western Australia and unfortunately has had no contact with me for many years. My first wife would not allow the girls to see me or make contact after the divorce, and for their sake, I was advised by the family court psychologist not to pursue the matter, as their mother would make their lives unbearable if they were in touch with me.

However, my elder daughter, Judy, is now very close. She has been married and divorced twice and is now a single parent with four children. She trained as a nurse and had an exceptional career caring for patients with heart, lung, and liver transplants at one of Melbourne's major hospitals. She gave this up to have children and to be a mum, but she still does nursing one or two days a week.

Life has been difficult for Judy, growing up with a mother that suffered from psychotic episodes and then marrying men who were most unsuitable. This has led to many emotional problems that Judy has had to cope with. We don't get to see each other all that often as we live on opposite sides of Melbourne, but phone and email connections are frequent. A close bond has developed between us, and we are there to support and help each other when needed.

Barbara's mum has lived with her for the last twenty-eight years, ever since her husband died under tragic circumstances. After an initial rocky start, I got along extremely well with Barbara's mum and we got to be very close. I actually knew her mum for more years than I had my own mum, who passed away when I was nineteen. But Barbara's mum could be difficult at times and was often very critical of those she loved the most. She often seems to lack warmth, and I have never seen her give Barbara a hug or a kiss, though no doubt she did when Barbara was a young child. This attitude became worse as dementia began to take over her brain. She also has macular degeneration and really hated the blindness that was slowly enveloping her.

But, for all the difficulties experienced with the personality clashes between Barbara and her mum, I have often heard Barbara say how grateful she was that her mum encouraged her to "be herself" when she was growing up. She was never told she could not do anything. As long as she wanted to do something and was prepared to put in the effort, "the sky was the limit." This belief that she could do anything she really wanted to is what has made Barbara such a strong person. It has helped her throughout her life and through this recent traumatic time.

Many of Barbara's friends and colleagues told her she would never be able to write this book, because of the disabilities she experienced after the stroke. But, as usual, she remained determined and has managed to reach her goal, even if more slowly than what she had planned.

I am very proud of Barbara, as are so many others. I am sure that her story will enthuse and motivate you. I am so pleased to be a part of her very special narrative.

CHAPTER 1

A Few Blinding Moments and My Life Was Changed Forever

My husband, Pete, my ninety-year-old mum, my son, Mark, and I made a "tree change" from living close to the city of Melbourne to moving to country Victoria. Drouin is now our hometown and is part of the beautiful, green, grassy, rolling hills of Gippsland. We are on two acres, which is also the home for many rabbits and hares. We love our flowers, trees, and large fountain fishpond, which has around forty fish that swim to me when I call them. They actually let me stroke them!

I also have two Cavalier King Charles Spaniel dogs. The elder, Cameo, is a Blenheim (red and white) female who is twelve years old, and the younger, Cooper, is a tricolour (black, white, and red) male aged five. Both enjoy being able to romp in such a large grassy area and especially like to bark at the rabbits when they dare trespass on their territory.

Thursday, May 19, 2011, started out like any other day. Little did I know that life as I knew it would never be the same. Pete and I had decided to do a small amount of grocery shopping. We did not like to shop during a weekday, as we both worked from home supporting the home based business operators and put in many long hours. We did not easily find time for such things as shopping.

On the way home, we noticed our neighbours had a car parked outside. As they both did shift work, we never quite knew when they would be home or if they would be sleeping or not. The car at the front of the house suggested that someone was home and not sleeping.

They had a new dog, which they had acquired when she was about five months of age, and she was difficult to walk. In fact, she had pulled my neighbour over and damaged her knee on a walk a few weeks before. The dog was now nearly a year old. As a dog judge, breeder, and trainer, I knew that the breed (border collie) was the most intelligent of all breeds, and I wanted to meet her and see if I could help the family with her training.

I knocked on the door and my neighbour invited us in to meet his dog. I did ten minutes of training and was sure the border collie would learn quickly with a bit of consistent training. We chatted a while and then left to go home for lunch.

I cook a hot meal at lunchtime as it best suits my mum. She is nearly blind from macular degeneration, has had cancer twice, has had her hip replaced twice, and uses a walking frame to help her get around the house. I am her official caregiver, or "carer," as I call it, and Pete and Mark, my son, help me to look after her.

I dished up the hot lunch for the others, but as I did not feel 100 percent, I only had a small bowl of soup. We decided to eat in the TV room and watch a show. My crab chowder soup smelled delicious, but I thought that it did not taste exactly as it should. I wondered why I seemed to lose my sense of taste. I had just finished my soup and placed the empty bowl on the coffee table when an unbelievably agonising pain engulfed me.

The pain in my head was like a sudden and unbearable explosion. It felt like a knife searing its way through my skull, twisting and stabbing at the same time. It grabbed me with so much ferocity that I could do nothing but hold my head and gasp for breath. I was drowning in pain. I could not speak. I could hardly think. I am sure I moaned as the all-consuming pain persisted. As the pain took over, I seemed to lose all sense of colour; everything was in black and white, with more black than white. I felt as though I were sinking into a massive black abyss. I desperately wanted to reach the light again.

"Are you okay?" Pete asked.

I thought, *What a silly question! Of course, I'm not okay!*

I could tell by the sound of Pete's voice that he was concerned and wanted to do something for me, but I just couldn't answer him. It took all my energy to tolerate the pain. I couldn't say a word. I couldn't even see his face; it was simply a blur.

After around ten minutes of the ghastly, agonising pain, Pete said, "I'm calling an ambulance."

I managed to mumble, "No!" I thought that the pain would subside and I would be okay in a few minutes. I didn't want to spend hours in a hospital, only to be told to take an analgesic and to rest.

Pete then asked me, "Do you think you have tic douloureux?" This is a facial neuralgia that I had had once before (many years ago), and the pain for that was also severe. Pete later told me that he thought that the intensity of the pain was very similar.

"What?" I gasped.

Again, Pete said, "Do you think you have tic douloureux?"

"I don't know what you're talking about," I muttered.

The pain had slightly eased and I was managing to relax a little. I was now more aware of what was going on around me. Pete again said, "I think I will call the ambulance."

"Do what you bloody like," I mumbled in utter desperation.

When the pain was at its worst and everything seemed darker and fuzzy, sound also seemed to be a long way off. I could not fathom what was happening to me. But now I felt things were returning to normal, and as I had stopped moaning and swaying, I was sure that I didn't need an ambulance; but if Pete wanted one, then so be it.

Pete later told me that he thought he knew what had happened to me when I did not understand when he mentioned tic douloureux, as not understanding what is being said is a well-known symptom of a stroke. However, such severe pain is not a classic stroke symptom, and that confused him. He immediately rang the ambulance, even though I was still sure that I did not need paramedics.

Little did I know that Pete's diagnosis was correct and that my life was about to change forever.

> When a friend or family member wants to get an ambulance for you, don't fight it. It is better to waste some time at the hospital if nothing is seriously wrong than to neglect what might be a significant or even life-threatening problem.

CHAPTER 2

Good News and Bad News

P ete disappeared. Later he told me that he went outside to guide the ambulance to our door, as the house numbering in our street is not the conventional "odds and evens" numbering. Being a cul-de-sac, the numbers all follow one another.

I was still sitting in my recliner chair in the TV room when the paramedics came and immediately asked me a number of questions. I was still feeling that it was unnecessary to have an ambulance, but I thought I should cooperate, as Pete was so concerned.

"Tell me what happened," the female paramedic said.

I struggled to say, "I suddenly had pain in my head."

"How long ago did the pain start?"

I had no idea. Pete said, "About twenty minutes ago."

"How would you describe the pain—one being not too bad and ten being really bad?"

"At its worst it was a ten; now it is about a six," I managed to say.

The female paramedic took my blood pressure and placed electrodes on me to take an ECG (electrocardiograph). A minute later, she checked the read-out. "Everything seems fine," she said.

As I looked at one of the paramedics, I remember thinking, *I don't think I have ever seen anyone look that tall.* He was like a giant; but then I wondered if he just appeared so tall because I was sitting down low in the recliner.

The tall paramedic then began to ask me more questions. "When is your birthday?"

"Eight, six, forty-four," I answered.

"Where are you?"

"At home."

"What is your address?"

I didn't know . . .

"What day is it?"

I didn't know . . .

"What year is it?"

I didn't know . . .

I found it difficult to respond to all these questions, as I felt confused and annoyed when I could not answer them. I thought, *It's amazing how pain can affect your memory.*

When I could not answer a question, the paramedics did not push me or react in any way that made me feel inadequate. They were kind, considerate, and gentle as they asked their questions and examined my vital signs. I began to relax a little.

While the paramedics were asking me these questions, I noticed Mum and Mark standing back at the entrance to the TV room where I was. They could see and hear what was happening. Mum was leaning on her walker and Mark had his arm around her shoulders. They looked so worried. I felt guilty for upsetting everyone. *After all, I've just got a bit of pain in my head*, I was thinking.

"I really do think you should go to the local hospital in Warragul for a doctor to examine you," the tall paramedic said.

Peter agreed with him, and I resigned myself to the fact that I would have to spend the next few hours in the emergency department.

The female paramedic then said, "I am going to put a cannula in your vein in case we need to give you medication either in the ambulance or in the hospital."

She tried to get it into the vein but was unsuccessful. This was nothing new for me; most medical people had trouble getting a cannula into my vein. They decided that I would have to wait to have the cannula put in at the hospital.

"Can you walk to the ambulance?" she asked.

I felt sure that I could stand and walk, but it took both paramedics, one on each side of me, to get me to the waiting ambulance. I felt weak and disoriented and found it difficult to walk in a straight line.

Finally, I was in the ambulance and strapped to the gurney. It took about fifteen minutes to arrive at the hospital, and I was surprised at how quickly a doctor saw me. Previously, when I had had to go to the emergency room with a kidney stone, I had to wait ages for a doctor.

Immediately, the doctor asked me the same sort of questions the paramedic had. "What is your name?"

"Barbara Gabogrecan."

"What is your date of birth?"

"Eight, six, forty-four."

"Who is the prime minister?"

Now I was really confused. "Do you mean all of Australia or here?" I asked.

I knew that the Australian federal government was Labor but the Victorian state government (where I lived) was Liberal and they had different political leaders. Which leader did the doctor want? It just had not registered with me that there was only one prime minister. I even wondered if the doctor had meant, "Who is the president?" I was just so confused and bewildered.

There were more questions.

"Where do you live?"

"Where are you now?"

But I couldn't answer them; I just could not seem to remember the names of the places and towns. Why was I so confused?

I remember thinking, *Ask Pete. He knows the answers!*

Dear Pete, he has always been important to me and so helpful in all aspects of my life. Even in those early moments of being in hospital, I was depending on Pete to make things right!

"I think we will leave the questions for now and send you for a CT scan," the doctor said.

I was wheeled out on my bed to have the CT scan (computerised tomography), which took about fifteen minutes, and then taken back to the emergency ward. Pete then told me that while I was gone, the doctor said to him, "I am pretty sure she has had a stroke."

Not too long after the scan, the doctor came back and said, "Well, I have good news and bad news. The good news is you have had a stroke, but it was a mild one. The bad news is we have also found a tumour on the brain."

My world suddenly tilted at a dramatic angle, yet strangely, I did not feel shock. I did not feel stressed or anxious either. I just felt confused. The doctor had just said that I had a brain tumour and a stroke, but that was good news? This seemed a bit odd to me. How could that be good news?

The confusion I felt was actually protecting me from fully comprehending what had just been explained to me. As it turned out, that was a good thing as it stopped me from experiencing any emotional collapse. This catastrophic news shook up Pete though. I could see the concern on his face as his eyes widened and his jaw seemed to drop.

Later, Pete told me just how devastated he felt; he said he could never have imagined me having a stroke, as I seemed so much in control of my life. But even now when I say to myself, "I have had a stroke and a brain tumour," it does not seem real; it feels as though I have simply imagined it. (I have always had a strong imagination.) It truly has been a surreal experience.

"What happens now?" I asked the doctor.

"We will send you to Monash hospital in Melbourne."

"When?" I asked, thinking I could probably go home now and a bed might become available in a couple of days.

"Immediately," was the doctor's response. "As soon as we can get an ambulance. We have rung Monash and they have a bed available for you now."

There was a delay in getting an ambulance to transport me, so Pete went home and packed a bag of essentials and told me he also put in a book for me to read, as we both loved reading. I hate the idea of being bored, so a book was a good standby.

While he was gone, I couldn't help but wonder, *Was the pain caused by the stroke or the brain tumour?* It was some days before it was fully explained to me what had happened.

Around five hours later, the ambulance arrived. Pete gave me a kiss and said he would be in to see me first thing in the morning. I was lifted onto the gurney and wheeled to the back of the ambulance. When I was finally inside and locked in, one of the ambulance officers joined me. We had over an hour's drive ahead of us and the officer tried to have a conversation with me, but he soon gave up as I could not remember things he was asking me. So he settled down and appeared to go to sleep.

I looked out through the large window in the back door and saw the night sky with blinking stars and the dark shadows of trees. As a kid, when I lived in the bush, on the occasional times we went to town, it was always late when we got home. My brother Jimmy and I would be lying down on the back seat of the tourer model Chev that Dad drove. Jimmy was sixteen months younger than me and he would be asleep in no time, but I would watch the sky and trees as we drove along. They fascinated me and always held a sense of mystery and beauty.

It was a pleasant late night drive for me on the way to Monash. I was not thinking of what had happened or indeed what might happen in the future. I was simply enjoying the night sky and my childhood memories.

In hindsight, I guess I should have felt worried, anxious, and even distraught. After all, I had just discovered that I had a life-threatening medical condition. A stroke would affect my ability to communicate effectively and therefore change my entire life as I knew it. But a tumour in the brain could mean that my life might be about to end. Yet I continued to feel strangely calm and relaxed.

1. When you arc in shock and trying to cope with a severe problem, try to fill your mind with happy, positive thoughts and don't dwell on "what if" worries.

2. Make the effort to keep a list of all medication that you take (including how much, how often, etc.), any allergies you may have, and all medical procedures you have had. Keep this list handy so that you can give it to paramedics, hospital emergency staff, and doctors together with your Medicare card, pension card, and ambulance membership card (if you have any of these).

This will save you a lot of time and angst when you are asked for this information during any medical emergency. Medical personnel have told me how helpful it was to receive this information, saying they wished that other patients would do the same.

CHAPTER 3

The Shock of My Life

I finally arrived at Monash hospital at one in the morning and was taken directly to the neurology ward. The room was lit by the soft glow of the emergency night lights. Everything was quiet and appeared to be peaceful.

A nurse came towards me and took my records from the paramedic. Because of the late hour, I thought they would speak in a whisper so as not to disturb sleeping patients. However, to my surprise, they spoke in normal tones.

My brain was idling in neutral as I was moved to a bed. Basically, I felt okay; there had not been any symptoms before the terrible pain to suggest that anything was wrong, and there were none now. I kept wondering, *Why don't I feel anything at all?* But there had been no warning signs, and now that the pain was gone, I began to think that everyone had overreacted.

Because I knew that all my body parts could move and I could still think, I wondered why I was even in hospital. If I felt anything at all, it was annoyance that I would lose valuable time from my work, and I worried how Pete could look after my mum without me. I felt that I should have been at home where I was needed.

Why I was not overpowered with fear at the thought that I had a brain tumour, I don't know. Perhaps it was the stroke that had made my brain act differently and not allowed me to fully comprehend what was happening, or perhaps it was just my nature not to worry about things over which I had no control.

While wheeling in my gurney and then getting me into the bed, taking my blood pressure, and checking my reflexes, the paramedics and nurse had made sufficient noise to disturb the other three patients in my room.

Soon after I was settled, one of the patients started crying out. Two nurses came rushing in, and I heard him say that the medication he had just been given was making him dizzy and disoriented. And he could not feel his legs

The nurses reacted very quickly to his complaints. They spent a fair amount of time testing the reflexes of his legs and feet. Eventually, they told him that nothing was wrong and his legs and feet were fine. He should just relax and try to sleep. While I was a patient in the neurology ward, I learned that one of the tests all nurses and doctors did to patients was to constantly test our hands and feet for reflexes and strength, as this could indicate more serious problems associated with the brain.

The disturbance was added to by a female patient next to me calling out, "Excuse me! I want a nurse!" The nurses told her she would need to wait as they were busy with the other patient, but she kept saying, "Excuse me . . . Excuse me." There was only a curtain between us, and there was no way I could ignore what was being said.

And apparently the third patient, who was opposite me, could not ignore it either. Things came to a head when he suddenly yelled out, "Shut up!"

I began to wonder if I would have been better off in my own bed at home and just come to hospital as a day patient, rather than be in this madhouse. I still could not accept that I was in serious trouble myself and needed constant medical attention.

I think I got about an hour's sleep that first night, before the nurses were checking my blood pressure and the reflexes in my limbs again. After these tests, I decided to get up and sit in a chair. It was about six in the morning, and as my back was aching, the chair seemed to offer some relief. It was then I decided to read the book that Pete had packed. It would keep me occupied until breakfast.

I took the book out of my bag and looked at the cover—it seemed both familiar and yet unrecognisable. I thought, *Have I already read this book?* I kept looking and tried to read the title and author, but I could not make any sense of it. Why? I then opened the book and again looked at the mad jumble of letters and thought, *Pete has bought a book written in another language, the silly goose!*

Pete had recently purchased quite a few books from Borders Bookstore, which was closing down and had lots of specials. But that didn't make any sense to me either. Why would Pete purchase a book written in another language? I really did not think he would make a mistake like that. So I concentrated really hard and finally recognised a single word: "the."

Then it hit me with a sudden thump. The book was written in English, but I couldn't read!

The shock of that realisation was unbearable. I was screaming inside, *No it cannot be! I have to be able to read. Please, God, make me able to read! Please...please...*

I was an author. Writing and reading were my major communication tools. I wrote all the content for my thirty-odd websites and blogs; I wrote books; I had a best seller. For crying out loud, I had just completed a book titled *How to Write an E-Book for Profit.* I had to be able to read!

This was more than I could bear. I burst into tears. Finally, I realised that something really terrible had happened to my brain.

Thoughts crowded through my head. If I could not read, did that mean that I could no longer run my home based business, where I offered support and mentoring to other business operators? I loved reading books, and now that pleasure was taken from me. I wondered if I could do the shopping if I could not read the labels on containers. Would I be able to drive if I could not read road signs?

It seemed that my life revolved around reading, yet it was something that I never really thought about. It was just as natural as breathing for me. For the first time since all this happened, I was forced to face the reality that what had happened to me was serious and that my life would never be the same.

A nurse came by and tried to console me, telling me that things would improve in time and not to panic as I would learn to cope.

"Come on, dry your tears and eat some breakfast," she said gently, pointing to my food that had just arrived. No doubt, the nurse had coped with many patients as they finally realised just how a stroke would affect their lives. It was a shock to accept that I was now one of those patients.

Once the initial panic was over, I sat for the next few hours and let my mind drift back to remember what my life used to be like. I also remembered another very difficult time for me when I was a child and we left the bush to live above a shop in the main street of Port Macquarie, a coastal town in New South Wales. This change in my life was a tough time too.

I was twelve and had to cope with so many new things that I was not used to. Having to attend school with my peers was simply awful. I was terrified of telephones and would actually hide in a cupboard when one rang. I even had to work in Dad's shop when it got busy and talk with dozens of strangers as I made them milkshakes and got their sweets or sandwiches.

There were no paddocks or animals; it was a total culture shock. The only way I could cope was to throw myself into my schoolwork, which I had always loved. It was difficult, but I finally adjusted and everything eventually turned out okay.

Was the catastrophe I was now facing going to be any different?

I had just had a horrifying shock, and after the first few hours, I knew without a doubt that I would need to throw myself into something that I could still do and that I loved doing, to boost my confidence and make me feel whole again. Just like I threw myself into my schoolwork when I was younger, I was sure I could do it again.

I believe that it is so important to think positively and set goals to strive for, to help you cope with shock and horror. The more you dwell on the negatives and the "Why me?" thoughts, the longer it will take you to recuperate. I made a decision. I had to find a way to be positive about this negative situation I found myself in. But this time, I had Pete to comfort me and to help my mind move forward with enthusiasm. I did not have this rock of strength to help me when I was twelve, so this time, I thought, it should be easier.

When things seem so bad that you cannot mentally cope, remember how you coped with other problems that you have had to face during your lifetime. Don't just dwell on how bad the other problems were but rather on how you coped and how the problems seemed less severe over time. Think positive and try to set some early goals that you can aim for.

CHAPTER 4

The Silver Lining

T he first day in Monash hospital was the beginning of my acceptance of the changes that I had to cope with. I kept thinking that there would no doubt be many more traumatic days in the weeks to come, and I wondered how well I would cope with them.

Pete arrived, and as we talked and he held my hand, he reminded me of a training program I had developed for home based businesses struggling to cope with everything. "You called it How Do You Eat an Elephant? Do you remember it?" he asked.

I did. The answer to the title's question was obviously "One bite at a time." To relate this title to small business, I changed the answer to "One step at a time."

"So, we will handle the problems you face one step at a time, Barb. Don't worry, it will be okay," Pete assured me.

I was quite teary at this time. I was so used to making Pete feel positive (he was by nature a pessimist) that I did not expect him to be propping me up now. But I was ever so grateful that he was able to.

We continued to talk, and it felt as though I had lost part of my memory—I couldn't remember the names of people or specific things. I remember asking Pete, "What is the name of my friend who looks after dead people?"

The name I was trying to remember was of a dear friend who is a civil celebrant specialising in funerals. What was strange was that I could remember the name of her new husband that I had only met a couple of times, yet I had known her for years. I could picture exactly what she looked like, where I had met her, and what we had done together. Indeed, I could remember everything—except her name.

With me constantly asking Pete questions like this, he became very good at working out what I was trying to remember.

Pete was with me for ten hours on that first day and was so tired he was falling asleep, while sitting in the chair with his head on my pillow and shoulder. However, just having Pete there with me made me feel safe. Everything was so unnaturally calm though, I wondered, *Is this the calm before the storm?*

Being Saturday, the specialist did not get to see me until Monday, but a staff doctor saw me and told me that I had to undergo a number of tests to see how severe the stroke had been and just what part of my brain had been affected. All sorts of tests took place during that first day in hospital, and the last one gave me some hope.

The first therapist asked me about my friends, what they did, and what their names were. She asked what I did for a living, what colour her shirt was, etc. At first, I was a little confused, but then I thought it was hardly like a test (it seemed more like a conversation), and finally I relaxed. However, the therapist was assessing everything I said and finally came to the conclusion that I had not lost my memory but that the damage from the stroke was such that my brain could not make letters form the words I needed.

She described it this way: "The brain sees letters grouped together to create words, and you are not recognising the words. You just see a jumble of letters." The problem, as she described it, seemed to me to be directly related to my inability to read rather than a memory problem.

Once the first therapist reached this conclusion, she sent a second therapist who proceeded to give me a lot of different tests. One test included her giving me a verbal description of objects and I had to tell her what they were. "What does a mother give her baby to suck to stop it from crying?" she asked.

"A dummy," I was able to answer.

Some I got right, like this one; others, I was unable to work out the answer.

Then I had to look at a series of pictures and say what was happening. They were pretty simple. I remember one was of a child holding an apple and talking to his mother who was washing dishes at the sink. I got most of these correct.

It really hit home how bad I was when the therapist asked me to name ten animals. I love animals and had many books on all kinds of animals, yet I was only able to respond with "A giraffe and an elephant." Then my mind went blank.

The therapist could see that my inability to answer this question was upsetting to me, and she said, "Don't worry. Just name some farm animals for me."

I had grown up on farms, so this should have been easy. But again, my brain would not cooperate. "A dog and a sheep" was all I could think to say.

I was devastated. How could this be? But the tests went on.

Next, I was shown a drawing of an object and I had to say what it was. I got most of them right, but there were two objects that appeared in both the verbal and pictorial tests that I just could not remember. One was a hammock and the other was a cactus. I still struggle with these two words. At first, it was so annoying and I was so determined to remember that I would ring Pete at home three or four times a day to ask him to help me. I would describe the object and ask him to give me the sound of the first letter.

"What is a plant that can grow in the desert and does not need much water?" I would ask.

It was no help if Pete told me it started with the letter c (pronounced "see"); he had to give me the sound of "k," and then sometimes I would get it right. If I didn't, he would have to tell me "cactus," I would repeat it three or four times, and then I would write it down. I have always believed that the brain remembers better if you do two or three associated tasks, such as read, listen, and write. However, even though I did this, an hour later I would have forgotten it again.

These tests demonstrated to me just how much brainpower I had lost, and I began to understand just what a challenge I was facing. The problem seemed to be not so much in recognising the object but rather working out the word to describe what I was observing.

As a dog judge, I had to learn the breed standards of many different breeds of dogs, and I decided to practise remembering the breeds after the therapist had left. I was managing to picture the individual dogs in my mind and even remember most of the breed standards—but I could not remember the names of the breeds I was picturing.

I owned and showed a wonderful little miniature schnauzer called Jimmy Joe. I could remember everything about him but could not remember what breed he was and even struggled with his name. This really upset me. It was one thing not to be able to remember names of objects the therapist showed me, but not to remember details of my beloved dogs was simply horrible.

One of the last tests the therapist gave me that day was to write my name. I did this successfully, though I thought it was wrong when I tried to read what I had just written; it *looked* wrong to me. But the therapist assured me it was correct.

The next day, a thought came to me. If I can still write, then someone else could read it back to me and help me with corrections; after all, I could write my name, so perhaps I could write a sentence. I grabbed some paper that Pete had packed in my bag with the book and I began to write.

I couldn't believe it. As I was writing, I could make sense of the words. Was the trauma over? I wrote my first line with growing excitement, but by the time I completed the second line of writing, I could not read the first line I had just written. There had been no "miracle cure" after all. I still could not read.

But I could write!

And write I did. I was on my third page when a group of surgeons came by. "What are you doing?" one asked.

"Writing," I answered with a happy heart.

"Does it make sense though?" the surgeon asked.

"I don't know," I responded. "You tell me. I can't read it!"

Each surgeon took my pages of writing to read and was obviously surprised that it made perfect sense. They concluded that I had the rare condition known as alexia without agraphia.

"Alexia means you cannot read. Agraphia means you cannot write. If you suffer from one you usually suffer from the other," the surgeon explained, "but you only suffer from alexia and not agraphia, which is a very rare phenomenon."

How cool is that? I thought with some glee. It was true; every cloud really does have a silver lining!

"Would you agree to us bringing student doctors in to give you some tests?" asked the surgeon.

Of course, I agreed. I was kept busy over the next week with a number of student doctors examining and testing me, so that they could see firsthand what they had previously only read about in a textbook.

I felt really chuffed that I could actually do something positive to not only help student doctors but also the future patients they would be looking after. It was good to know that my suffering wasn't all in vain and that it did offer some useful side benefits.

Being kept so busy and with Pete there to support me, I felt my spirits rise and my confidence coming back. Perhaps the future was not going to be so bleak after all.

There is always a silver lining—you just have to find it. Keep looking and remain positive, and it will be easier to find. Often the silver lining is not evident or might not be obvious. It can appear to be small and insignificant, but it is there just waiting for you to find it. Sometimes, it can even be found in others, depending on what their needs are.

CHAPTER 5

Why Me?

I accepted that I had to take constant positive steps if I was to avoid falling into an abyss of self-pity. I was quite fragile at this time and was aware that only my inner strength was going to bring me through this ordeal. I knew it would be a real battle to remain positive.

It is one thing to be positive when everything is moving along at an exciting pace; it is quite another thing to be positive when you are in a stressful situation like I was at this time.

I call myself a "realistic optimist"; I am confident that the best will happen but like to be prepared for the worst, in case that is the outcome. That is why I was so devastated when I found I could not read—I wasn't prepared for that. I must admit, of everything that happened to me over the next few weeks, not being able to read was the most traumatic experience of all.

To help me be positive, Pete made a list of what I could still do that I loved doing and that would not depend on me being able to read. The first two that came to mind were artwork and dog training.

Being able to write created a real moment of elation for me, relief, and yes, excitement. So, while in this positive frame of mind, making a list with Pete seemed like a very good idea. My competitive spirit and being prepared to "give it a go" has often led to success and joy for me, and I had to make sure that this attitude remained with me as I struggled with the effects of both the stroke and the brain tumour.

People have asked me, "Did you ask yourself, 'Why me?'" I can honestly say, "No." Really, why not me?

My experience is that it is too easy to blame someone or something for the problems and the adversity we have to face. Fate has a way of levelling out the playing field of life. Sometimes, life is good; sometimes it is bad. I think we have to learn to accept and cope with whatever is dealt to us if we want to be happy with our life.

During that first week, I realised that I had to be prepared to give up what I was used to doing and be able to accept that I might have to start my life again from scratch. I assumed that I would not be able to do everything that I had been doing: running my business, using the computer, mentoring business owners, etc.

It was difficult to acknowledge that I could be losing everything I had built my adult life around and loved doing. However, at the same time, I knew from experience that other positive and rewarding opportunities would arise. They always had in the past, and I just had to make sure that I was prepared to recognise and accept them.

My character has a strength that has helped me overcome many problems and heartaches in the past. It is my ability to put aside what I no longer have and simply move on and concentrate on what I do have, that has given me such a fulfilling life. I am very capable of creating completely new and positive scenarios that can supersede previous circumstances.

I have been quite independent for many years. In the past, I have not turned to or relied on friends or family in times of trauma or need. It took many years for me to trust Pete enough to depend on him. Somehow, I felt that if I depended on others, they would eventually let me down, which would lead to me experiencing heartache and misery. Being independent seemed much safer and therefore more appealing.

But this blow that fate had handed me was about to change my life and I needed a new direction, so I started to think about the list that Pete made for me. *What could I still do that I liked doing?*

Mmmm, I was pleased that I was thinking in terms of what I *liked* doing—it must be my old age kicking in and the realisation that you have to enjoy what you are doing if you want to be truly happy and feel as though you have a worthwhile purpose in life.

I could still paint, so perhaps I could go back to painting full time. After all, that was where my career path in business had begun. I went from being an art teacher to producing my art designs on product suitable for the tourist market. I was very successful in a very short span of time. Winning seven Australian Gift of the Year Awards was a major achievement in the first two years of my art business, which gained a lot of publicity for me. When I had my designs produced under licence by sixteen significant manufacturers, such as Shelta Umbrellas, Fresca Scarves, and Laurentino Bags, I was assured of the popularity of my designs. My business began to flourish and proved to be an exciting and rewarding time in my life.

One of the reasons that I had slowed my painting down over the last few years was because my fingers and back were suffering from rheumatics, and this meant that I could only paint for short periods at a time before the pain would stop me. Consequently, production was slow and hardly profitable now. I wasn't so sure that painting was going to be the answer. Nevertheless, at this time of trying to decide what I could still manage, painting was right up there at the top of the list.

Also at the top of the list, I placed training dogs—they didn't care if I could read or not. Perhaps I could get a new puppy and start training it. But I knew that even training dogs had its limitations for me. I found it difficult to bend down to the dogs' height (the rheumatic problem again), and this affected my training abilities. I had been unable to walk Cameo and Cooper for some time now, as I was waiting to have a second hip replaced and the pain caused by walking was quite debilitating. Consequently, I had been going to hydrotherapy to keep my muscles moving and supple. I wished I could take the dogs to swim with me!

However, on the TV show *The Dog Whisperer*, I saw a man in a wheelchair with crippled hands train two pit bull dogs to walk beside him without pulling, to lie beside him without being over excited, and to generally behave as "good citizens." I figured if a man with these disabilities could train such a difficult breed of dog, then surely I could train my dogs to do tricks and to be service dogs. In the back of my mind, I was considering training both dogs to make hospital visits. That seemed like a worthwhile challenge.

Fortunately, most of the time, I was able to speak quite well and what I said made sense. Occasionally, I needed help with an elusive word and Pete was there to help me. I had given lots of presentations over the years, so why not offer a motivational talk to describe not only what had happened to me but how I coped? This could help others who suffered similar health issues to remain positive and motivated. It could also help those who had loved ones suffering to better understand what they needed to do to help them. This too seemed like a worthwhile option.

It was vitally important to me, in those early days, to force my mind to consider options that would keep me feeling worthwhile and productive. The optimism began to kick in. I just knew that I could still lead a satisfying life. But I also wanted to make an income and I wondered how to do that, as motivational speaking would have to be free of charge.

Then I realised that part of my presentation would be based on how to cope with that very problem: how to remain productive and earn an income. Then I thought of a possibility. Why not have some of my products available for sale at the presentations? I had books, silk scarves, and cards that were created from photos of my dogs. I was sure a number of people attending my presentations would want to buy some of these products. After all, I was already selling my products to the general public via my website, so I knew they were of a high standard and in demand.

I was feeling pretty optimistic about it all as the creative side of my mind kicked in. I knew that being constructive, having goals, and accepting challenges would definitely be a way to improve my well-being and build my inner strength.

When I do meet people who only think of themselves and their own problems, who constantly say, "Why me?" or "It is not fair," I say to them, "Take your mind off your problems and spend some time helping others cope with theirs."

This attitude made me much more capable of coping with the seemingly overwhelming and soul-wrenching happenings in my own private world and forced me to consider the bigger picture. Caring for others before caring for myself has proven to be an all-important step in the development of my psyche.

It was at this time that I began to worry about Pete rather than myself. Pete was making the one hundred kilometre trip to Monash hospital each day from our home in Drouin, and I knew it was exhausting him; as I could see dark circles appearing around his eyes, and his whole body seemed to sag. Looking after my mum, doing the laundry, preparing meals, feeding and grooming the dogs, gathering things to bring in to me, and then making the daily trip to the hospital and back had become a huge burden for him. Our home based business also suffered, as Pete was unable to spend any time on running the business.

"Stay home tomorrow and have a rest," I said to him on a number of occasions. "I'll be okay."

"I'm fine," Pete would answer, "and I want to be here with you."

Pete was determined to give me as much support and encouragement as he could. Working through the list he had made of things I could do became an important activity for us both. While I was trying to think of all the things I could do, it took Pete to think of the realities.

When we were discussing painting as a possible option, Pete asked me, "Are you sure you can still paint on silk?"

Silk was my chosen medium for painting, but it did require some very specific skills. I have to draw on the silk by using a small plastic tube of gutta, which is a liquid rubber that acts as a barrier so that the coloured dyes will not flow together. I have to apply a constant pressure on the plastic tube to make the gutta flow evenly. At the same time, I need to keep my hand steady without applying too much pressure on the silk; otherwise, I might puncture it with the needle-like tip and leave a hole.

I looked at Pete questioningly as this thought penetrated my mind. "Well, no. I'm not sure."

Then other thoughts raced through my mind. What if I did not remember my colours or I could not hold the brush? What if I could not even draw? But Pete knew how to help me get over my mental hurdle, as the very next day he arrived with paper, a small container for water, brushes, and special coloured pencils that, when used with water, give the effect of paint.

My bed was next to a window and was two stories above the ground, but I could see some plants growing below. It did not take me long to start drawing and then to paint the scene.

I spent some time observing the shape of the plants and looking at the negative space, or background spaces, as shapes. This technique is a trademark of my art. Then I completed a drawing using a black pen. I was quite happy with the results but tired very quickly.

The next day I tried again, this time using the coloured pencils, brush, and water. The result was pretty basic, but nevertheless, I now knew that I could manage both drawing and colour. I would not know if I could use the gutta pen until I was at home. If I couldn't, then I would simply have to change my medium!

I find that it is so important to think of alternative scenarios when being faced with a problem. While recovering from my stroke, I was aware that it would be easy to just give in because I could no longer do what I used to. But I believe there is always another way to achieve what I want in life, and recovering from a stroke is no different. I had to accept what I could not do and concentrate on what I could do. But most importantly, I knew that I had to feel good about the new challenges I now had to face.

It was very important to me that I had the support of Pete to encourage and assist me by providing the skills that I did not have, mainly the memory and reading ability. This would ensure that I remained focussed and determined. It would be this combined effort that would bring me the rewards and results that I was aiming for.

But still I felt that there was "something" missing. I needed a spark to ignite my enthusiasm. I needed to motivate myself to a higher level of participation. I needed a super exciting goal to work towards.

Suddenly, I had an unbelievable brain wave! I would write a book titled *Thank God I Had a Stroke.* The title was obvious to me. If I hadn't had the stroke, then they might not have discovered that I had a brain tumour until it was too late. This was the "something" I could throw myself into—it was what I had been looking for.

As I couldn't read, this seemed like an impossible goal. But as soon as the thought came to me, I knew I could do it. I thrived on this type of challenge, and at this time, there was hardly anything I could think of that could be more challenging.

I was so excited by the idea. This was my true optimistic spirit I could feel bubbling around inside me. I love this quote from Zig Ziglar, as it seemed to exactly fit my life at this moment "Things turn out the best for those who make the best of how things turn out." How true this was for me.

1. As quickly as possible after the onset of your illness, set yourself goals to aim for. They needn't be huge, but you do need to have some. Concentrate on reaching these goals and encourage your family to help motivate you towards reaching them. Think about what you can do, not what you can't do.

2. I realise that doctors don't want to scare patients, but it would be helpful if patients were quickly made fully aware of the possible problems they might have to face. This could then mitigate the shock to the patient who discovers any traumatic results by himself or herself.

CHAPTER 6

I Moved to a Hotel

I wondered if time would improve my reading skills, as many had suggested. I don't know, but if this was how I was to be, then I had to accept it. I believe that it is a waste of time and energy to fight something over which you have no control. It is better to accept and cope with these things. So that is what I did. After all, I knew that what I was experiencing was so much better than what it might have been.

During this time, I was exercising by walking around the ward three times a day and quickly built up the laps from three to eight each time.

There were notices on the walls and signs above the walkway. Each time I passed them, I tried to read them, but they made no sense. Then one day, I suddenly recognised that one of the words on a sign said, "Stroke." I said to a nurse who was approaching, "Can you please tell me what that sign says?" She informed me that the sign was listing what the ward specialised in: patients who had neurological disorders including a stroke.

Wow—that was an exciting moment for me! If I could read one word, how long would it take me before I could read a sentence? Perhaps what I had been told about slowly improving was correct. The improvement was happening; my brain was trying to heal itself. It seemed as though I had nothing to worry about—nothing, that is, except a tumour on the brain!

When I wasn't walking around the ward, I was sitting in my chair (usually with Pete beside me) while working out how to manage the home and imagining what the future would be like. I was feeling more and more self-reliant each day.

Early on the morning of the fourth day (before Pete had arrived), a nurse came to me and said, "You are doing very well and are no longer considered to be a bed patient, so we are sending you to the Medi Hotel."

This sounded interesting. I wondered just where it was and if Pete would be able to find me when he arrived. It turned out to be a part of the same ward I was in and was simply separated by a door in the corridor.

This part of the hospital was designed to give patients a more pleasant and more natural environment, where they could build up their strength and prepare for going home.

Patients were expected to do a lot to look after themselves. There was only one nurse for the sixteen patients in the Medi Hotel. However, in the case of an emergency, more staff were immediately available, as they simply had to come through the door.

Like the other wards, there were four beds to a room, but instead of curtains all around, there was a solid wall that reached three quarters of the way to the ceiling. This separated each bed. The curtains were in the front only. It wasn't really more private, but it gave the impression of privacy. The floors were carpeted, and patients were expected to make their own beds.

There was a kitchen/dining room where you were to prepare your own breakfast of cereal, bread, and spreads that were provided. The lunches and dinners were brought from the main kitchen to this room, where we sat and ate. As hospital food is often cold by the time it reaches you, the microwave was very popular. There was cold, filtered water and hot water for tea available at any time. Patients simply had to stack dirty dishes in a dishwasher and leave the area tidy.

I liked the Medi Hotel and felt more relaxed and less stressed. It seemed to provide sanctuary and a sense of safety, a place where you could relax and boost your spirit.

My surgeon, Mr. Bala, who was to remove the brain tumour, arrived the day I entered the Medi Hotel and introduced himself to me. He was a young, very good-looking guy who had a calm, quiet manner and gave me the impression of being a very caring person.

He told me that my tumour was pressing against the brainstem and recommended that it be removed. He cautioned me though that this was a very serious operation, as the tumour was deep in the centre of the brain (seven centimetres, in fact) and was relatively large (three centimetres). It would be my decision as to whether to go ahead with surgery or try radiation to see if they could reduce the size of the tumour to take the pressure off the brainstem.

I wanted Pete to hear the prognosis and to see what he thought, even though I knew I wanted the tumour removed as quickly as possible. When Pete came to visit later that day, Mr. Bala came back to discuss it with both of us. He also told us that the pain I had experienced was called trigeminal neuralgia and was caused by the tumour. Now I knew what had caused the pain, and it wasn't the stroke.

Pete was on the right track when he initially thought it might be tic douloureux (a facial neuralgia). It just so happened that while I was experiencing the pain, I also had a stroke. But the two were not connected to each other; apparently, one had not caused the other, as I initially thought.

There was no discussion needed or time for Pete and me to "think about it"; we both wanted surgery as soon as possible. So I was scheduled for two weeks later.

Like most people, I have faced many problems in my life. Some of them have seemed insurmountable, while others are relatively minor but at the time did not seem that way. This time, nature had dealt me a blow, but I could not afford to be swamped with negative thoughts. I had to remain positive. But I could not help wonder, *What is going to happen to me now?* Was I about to go through a trauma that would deflate me entirely, or would I again be able to start a whole new life with enthusiasm and excitement?

Because I had also had a stroke, Mr. Bala wanted to be as sure as possible that I did not have another stroke during the lengthy brain surgery. He decided that I needed a blood thinner to reduce the risk. However, that could cause a problem of excessive bleeding during surgery. It posed a quandary for the medical team.

Initially, I was given two injections in the stomach, daily, of a mild blood thinner that would not permanently thin the blood and could be stopped three days before the operation.

Next, Mr. Bala needed an MRI (magnetic resonance imaging) to give him better knowledge of just exactly where the tumour was positioned, so he could work out how to remove it with as little risk of any permanent brain damage as possible.

"What are the side effects I could expect from the surgery?" I asked in a quiet voice.

"You are likely to have a droop on the left side of your face, which should improve, but it may be permanent," he replied. "You could also lose the use of your right arm and leg," he added.

I had just lost the ability to read and was delighted to realise that I could still write. Now it was being suggested that my right hand might be damaged, which could stop me from writing! However, I refused to give in to these negative thoughts. I remained determined to be positive and began to think of alternative solutions, such as computer software that could convert talking into writing, if needed.

There was no question that my mind continuously thought about how to cope and move forward, regardless of what challenge I was forced to face. I felt that I had actually set the biggest challenge I faced: my commitment to write a book. Once I made my mind up, nothing was going to stop me. The fact that I might not be able to read or write was not going to be a deterrent either. Somehow, I would find a way.

I have never been a patient person. I love to move forward with purpose and enthusiasm so that I can quickly reach my goals. I hate wasting time and procrastination.

My time in hospital certainly forced me to be tolerant, patient, and more relaxed, while I waited for the medical wheels to grind into action. I realised that if I could not relax, it might well delay my recovery.

I heard a number of patients crying or demanding action, just because they had to wait. One lass said to the specialist, between her tears, "I was told I would have the test yesterday. I am still waiting. I want to go home to my children. I don't want to wait any longer."

The third time the doctor saw her and she repeated the same complaint, the doctor said, "This is a public hospital and you just have to wait. We have many patients, and they all have to wait. So calm down; we will complete your tests as soon as we can."

Being patient was indeed a virtue that saved me from a great deal of angst. I was sure that having patience would help lead me to a successful and speedy recovery, and I have found it a great tool in my personal life, in business, and now in hospital. I had a serious medical condition and it was very important for me to concentrate on my ability to handle stress and stay calm. I knew that if I was not patient, the seriousness of my condition could be exacerbated.

Developing a definite routine helped me remain patient while in the Medi Hotel. I had an early-morning shower and then listened to some music with a player and headphones that Pete had brought in for me. After breakfast, I would do my walking around the hospital ward and then write three or four pages (like a diary), and Pete would read them to me when he arrived. Next, I would listen to my music again until about an hour before lunch when I would walk another few laps and then watch a TV show. After lunch, I would watch another TV show. I discovered that there are some great old classic shows on during daytime TV, which I had never realised as I don't normally watch TV at that time. Then I would lie down for a rest while listening to my music again until Pete arrived.

I had never just listened to music before. I always did something else while the music was playing. Now I just listened to the music and was really enjoying the experience. Pete usually arrived about 2.00 p.m. each day and we just had some quality time together. We talked or just sat silently and enjoyed each other's company while holding hands.

I was receiving literally hundreds of emails (mainly from business associates) wishing me well, and Pete would print them off and read them to me. This was indeed a blessing, as it kept me mentally and emotionally in touch with my business life and was a tangible connection with an important part of my life that I was afraid I might lose.

It all seemed so surreal. I was really resting, as I was not stressed or worried about anything. I had made peace with myself, and thanks to Pete's calmness too, I was nearly enjoying the Medi Hotel experience. I sensed that it was so important to feel calm and relaxed when leading up to major surgery.

Don't fret and become intolerant of hospital life. If you need to be there, accept that it is for your own good. Take an interest in other patients and see if you can make them feel better. Set an example and be a role model.

Also, consider and respect staff that are doing their best to look after you. Don't complain all the time; try thanking them and telling them how much you appreciate them. This can go a long way in making your stay in hospital more bearable.

CHAPTER 7

Building Bridges

A s the extra time I spent in the Medi Hotel ward did force me to rest, I was calm enough not to worry about what was to happen, or indeed, what had already happened. I continued to feel relaxed and enjoyed the routine as well as getting to know some of my fellow patients.

It was difficult to form relationships with the patients I came into contact with, as they moved in and out of hospital in very short time frames.

One fellow patient who stands out in my mind is Geoff. We met (as most of us did at the Medi Hotel) in the kitchen. He was keen to show me, and indeed all new patients, "the ropes." He would point out where the cutlery, bread, spreads, etc. were. When his meals arrived, he would ask us all if we wanted his dessert. He had a habit of storing them in the fridge to eat them later but would happily give one to anyone who wanted it. There always seemed to be a stack of his goodies still in the fridge. I guess it was his generous and caring nature that drew me to him.

Geoff told me that he had a brain tumour removed about ten years ago and it had regrown. This time there was nothing the doctors could do and he was told he probably had about a year to live.

I guess Geoff was in his late fifties and unfortunately had nowhere to live. Consequently, he had been in the Medi Hotel for some months and had walked the entire hospital many times, so he really knew his way around.

As I previously mentioned, nurses usually had difficulty getting a needle into my vein to take blood, as my veins would collapse or move when the needle was inserted. While in the Medi Hotel, I had to have a blood test, and when two nurses tried and failed, they decided I needed to go downstairs to the phlebotomy nurses who specialised in taking blood. When I was in the main ward, these nurses would come to me, but as I was in the Medi Hotel, I now had to go to them.

This created a dilemma, as I could not read. I couldn't work out where to go by reading the printed signs and I could not remember words, so I could not ask for guidance from anyone either. I still struggle to remember the words *Medi Hotel*. When I explained this to the nurse, she thought for a minute and then asked Geoff if he would take me.

In keeping with his generous spirit, Geoff was happy to guide me. During the hour-long wait, we chatted. I am not sure how accurate Geoff was with his story, because his brain, like mine, was not operating as it should, but he told me that his family did not visit him or keep in touch. Apparently, he had an old, rundown house that was literally falling apart, on a small property. One brother who lived interstate had come to see him soon after he was told he only had a year to live and tried to organise Geoff to give him power of attorney. Geoff would not do this, and he hadn't heard from that brother since.

Because Geoff had to be looked after, the hospital decided to keep him at the Medi Hotel until a permanent care residence could be found. At one point, he said to me, "I wish I had a little bit of money because I would like to buy a watch." I remembered that Pete had a watch that he did not use and I asked him if he would like to give it to Geoff. Of course, he said, "Yes."

Then, as so often happens in hospital, a nurse came to Geoff in the kitchen and said, "We have found a home for you, Geoff.

You had best go and pack your belongings now as someone will come and pick you up in a couple of hours."

Geoff was excited, yet at the same time nervous. He had felt secure and well looked after in the Medi Hotel and wondered what the new home would be like. Off he went with hope in his heart that all would be fine. I did get the address details of where he was going, and Pete and I decided, when I was fit enough, that we would be his regular visitors and even take him on short trips if he would like.

I have always believed that if you really want to get better from any illness (from depression to a brain tumour and everything in between), then you must avoid boredom at any cost. I had no doubt that Geoff would not find time to get bored as he settled into his new home.

I also got to know two young women while in the Medi Hotel. They were there because they were experiencing pregnancy problems and had to have complete bed rest. Most of the time, they stayed in bed watching TV, but they would come to the kitchen for their meals and I would get to talk with them. One of the things I asked them was what they with their time to keep from getting bored.

"Just watch TV and read some magazines," was their reply.

I just could not imagine doing that for months while waiting for the baby to arrive. "What are your hobbies?" I asked.

"We don't have hobbies," was their reply. They simply had done the housework, read magazines, and watched TV before they came to hospital.

I found this so hard to understand. They actually did not sound as though they were happy doing so little but just accepted that was what they did and would continue to do. Though having a baby would give them more to occupy themselves in the future.

I had always thought that the worst thing that could happen to me was to be bored. After the stroke, I had worked out what I could still do, as I *needed* to be fully occupied with meaningful and interesting activities that would allow me to stretch my mind and be productive. I wanted to make an income too, though if that was not possible now, I could still be happy if I could fulfil my dream of being active and helping others.

For me, to keep my spirits up and remain positive, I must ensure that I also keep my mind busy, even though it was my brain that was damaged. It would have been so easy for me to just give in and do nothing, blaming nature and everyone else for my condition. But to do nothing would have made me bored, and I am afraid of boredom.

The many activities I was involved in included painting, writing books, designing websites, doing presentations, training and judging dogs, organising events (including major awards), training people on how to run a business, sitting on government committees, being president of two associations, making DVDs and CDs, and reading. I was always busy with a wide variety of activities and could not imagine anything less. It is just not in my genes to do nothing; I must be active if I want to be happy.

I guess I felt sorry for the pregnant ladies. To me, their lives seemed so empty. Then I wondered if my life would be empty too if I found that I could not do many of the activities that I was involved in prior to the stroke. Was I about to suffer from a sense of feeling useless? Or would I learn to enjoy working more slowly and be satisfied with what I could still manage? I thought if the only thing I could do was to help people like Geoff, then I would still feel fulfilled and my life would not be wasted.

I did get quite a few visitors when I was in hospital, but I was amazed when my youngest brother, Fred, came to visit. He has always been regarded as the "black sheep" of the family, and we seldom saw or even heard from him. Sometimes, he would ring Mum when it was Mother's Day or Christmas, but other than that, I had seen him only twice since he had reached adulthood. Once was at Dad's funeral twenty-eight years earlier and once was when he visited me to see Mum about nine years ago.

Fred always had some extraordinary jobs throughout his life, such as jumping from a helicopter with his dog to earmark wild buffalo in the outback. He was a good cook, and like my dad, he was self-taught, so he often worked on stations as the cook. Whatever he did, it was always in the bush, and I am just amazed he survived all the dangerous activities.

He had put on some weight, but he looked good. Unfortunately, Fred was virtually an alcoholic, but he had recently given up the drink as he had been diagnosed with pancreatitis. A doctor had told him that he could die if he didn't give up alcohol. He seemed a lot better for this change.

Fred came in with Pete to see me, three days running. As Pete was spending around six hours a day with me, Fred did too, and we had some really great chats. After all, we had a lot of catching up to do.

When it was mealtime, both Pete and Fred would go to the very good cafeteria at Monash and get their meals and then bring them back to join me with my meal. After we had eaten our meals, many of the patients got to know each other by swapping yarns and discussing our concerns. It was sort of therapeutic to be able to open up to virtual strangers who, in all probability, we would never see again. Perhaps it was because we were all in the neurology ward and experienced similar problems that we were so open with each other.

One of the days Fred visited me, we got to talking about birthdays, as mine was coming up the following week. Fred told us the story of once when it was his birthday and his boss sent him into the town to collect some gear, and while there, another mate gave him a slab of beer.

He was drinking the beer while driving back to the property that night. He became tired and decided to pull up to the side of the road and have a sleep. He simply laid out his sleeping bag beside his car and went to sleep. But it must have been more like losing consciousness, as when he woke in the morning he saw tyre marks across the top of his sleeping bag. A road train had driven past during the night and the wheels had actually driven over his sleeping bag only a couple of inches from his head. He had not heard anything.

Fred had also nearly given up smoking—but not quite. It was an issue on smoking that made him mad with me during his visit, though he only let Pete know how annoyed he really was. He didn't want to upset me.

A fellow patient who had had back surgery had her bed between my bed and the window. We were separated by the three-quarter-inch wall, which gave a semblance of privacy. She was a happy soul and often could not help herself as she laughed out loud at something my visitors and I would say. It was like having an imaginary friend in our discussion, but we could not get annoyed when she participated in our chat, as she was so jolly.

She found it painful to sit, so when she came into the kitchen, she would stand to eat or talk to us. One day the topic of smoking came up, and she admitted that she was a smoker but would dearly love to give it up.

Now smoking is one of the vices that get me riled up, as I just can't accept that people put their lives at risk by continuing to smoke, often when they are already suffering from a smoking-related condition like emphysema or cancer.

Pete was a heavy smoker before I met him and developed what he thought was a cold sore on his lip. It would not heal, and finally he went to a doctor who immediately sent him to a specialist. It was a cancer, and he was operated on the next day. It was radical surgery that lost him his bottom lip. Plastic surgery techniques allowed his top lip to be cut to create the two lips, but his mouth was left much smaller than it was originally.

The cancer was so close to his lymph glands that the surgeon said if he had waited another week, Pete might not have survived. He was told that if he didn't give up smoking he would be lucky to survive another year. Consequently, he never smoked again.

I nearly feel as though I have a mission to convince smokers to give it up. I don't know how successful I am, but I no longer feel guilty about being blunt and even brutal when discussing smoking issues with smokers. It is no longer just their business.

It is everyone's business. The cost of hospital care for smoking-related conditions is unbelievable and uses up our scarce health-system resources that could be put to better use. Yes, I do get riled when discussing smoking!

Those of us in the kitchen that day had a lively discussion, and I tried to use my psychology training to help my roommate gather the strength and motivation she needed to give up this ghastly habit. Fred thought I was much too harsh and should leave her alone. Perhaps what I was saying was a bit too close to home for him, as he had not entirely given up smoking himself. Pete told me that on his drive home that night, Fred vented his anger at how blunt I was and felt that it was none of my business and I should "butt out."

However, the next day when my roommate was going home, she came to see me to thank me for the discussion. She was going to try again to give up smoking, as she had not smoked while in hospital. She said, "Last night, what you had to say made me think what a fool I am, and you made me determined to have a serious go at giving up smoking. Thank you."

I do hope my roommate was successful in giving up her "dirty and deadly habit."

All patients in the neurology ward were in a similar condition, and I felt blessed that I was able to develop short-term relationships and support fellow patients, regardless of how fragile we all were. I really believe it helped me to overcome my own concerns by being able to concentrate on the problems that my fellow patients faced. I do think that when I consider others before myself, it gives me an inner strength that helps me cope with my own fragility.

Consider telling interesting and humorous stories to other patients. Take their minds (and yours) off the problems you are all personally facing. An interesting story is always good for the soul.

CHAPTER 8

The MRI Madness

I t wasn't only me and my fellow patients who were frail. It turned out that Pete was fast becoming fragile as well.

As Pete did not come to visit me until after he had gotten Mum her lunch, he would ring to say good morning. I had difficulty remembering his phone number, so he wrote it on a large label and stuck it on the back of my phone, so that I could ring him too. Even then, I would often get one of the numbers wrong and would find myself talking to some poor, unsuspecting stranger.

I soon became the one to ring Pete to say good morning, as I would get impatient waiting for him to call me. Even though I did not ring too early, he was still in bed no matter at what time I called. Often it was after 10.00 a.m. when I rang, and I was still waking him up. This concerned me, as I thought that he might be sliding into depression. Pete suffered from depression from time to time and was on a mild form of medication for it.

One morning when I rang, Pete said, "I don't think I will come in today, if you don't mind, love."

Of course, I didn't mind, but I asked, "Why? What's wrong?"

"My back is pretty sore and I think I should rest it, and then I'll be okay to see you tomorrow."

I was worried, but often a day of bed rest would enable him to function and move around the next day. But not this time. He was taking painkillers and muscle relaxants and only able to struggle out of bed to feed the dogs and get Mum her meals.

Pete remained in this condition for three days, and all our communication was by phone. It was during this time that I was seen by a number of different doctors, preparing me for the next step in my journey. Consequently, I had news to share with Pete every time I rang him.

"I wish I could be there to hear what the doctors have to say," Pete said.

"I wish you were too," I replied. "I have difficulty remembering everything they tell me, and you would better understand them and could discuss everything with me later on."

I was in some sort of a haze and my memory remained foggy. There is no doubt that I would have better understood what they were telling me if Pete could have been with me at this time.

I wondered how patients managed to follow what doctors told them when they were on their own and did not have the support that I normally had via Pete.

One of the things I liked about Monash hospital was that the doctors obviously worked in teams and the more experienced doctors were always a part of the team that visited me. Around five doctors came to each patient every morning to ask how we were going and to do some checks on us and answer our questions. They also had regular team meetings to discuss each patient and how best to deal with our problems.

One of the doctors who had visited me told me he was a consultant and was advising the other doctors on the best action to take with me. He commented, "You are the most popular patient we have at the moment, because you have two teams discussing you: one for the stroke and another for the tumour. Then the two teams have to get together and discuss you again, to ensure that the treatment from one team does not negate what the other team is going to do."

Somehow, I think I would have preferred to be popular for a different reason.

All my doctors agreed that as soon as the MRI was completed, I could go home and have two weeks to rest before surgery. Well, that was easier said than done. Every day for the next week, I was told, "Tomorrow you will get the MRI." But each day, there were patients more critical than me needing the MRI and there just were not enough machines to handle the numbers of patients waiting. I thought that if it was me who needed an MRI urgently and I was made to wait my turn, I would not be very happy. So I was thankful the hospital prioritised its treatment in this way.

As well as waiting for an MRI, I was also waiting for an echocardiogram to test how well my heart was doing. Instead of me having to go to where the machine was, it was brought to me. When it finally arrived to do the tests, it took nearly an hour.

"Can you see anything that could cause me a problem when I am operated on?" I asked.

"Well, it is looking pretty good to me," the technician responded. "But we need the specialist to have a look and make sure everything is okay."

That was good news that she thought everything looked okay, because I had suffered from AF (atrial fibrillation) for over twenty years. My heartbeat jumped around, which meant that not all of the blood was pumped out of my heart as it should be and it could thicken in the heart. The doctors thought this thickening of the blood might have caused a clot to form, which in turn caused the stroke. So it was pretty important for me to have my heart working as well as it could for the surgery.

Many of the delays for an MRI were caused by patients freaking out at the idea of having a shield put over their faces and having to go into a tight, narrow tube. They would simply panic and could not stay there. Consequently, they had to be sedated and a doctor had to give the injection. This added a huge amount of time to the already tight schedules the MRI team was trying to meet.

Eventually, Mr. Bala managed to convince the MRI team to "fit me in," as we were getting close to the operation date and he needed to have the results well before he commenced the surgery. My two weeks at home resting was reduced to one week. Thank goodness, I was able to rest while waiting in the Medi Hotel.

Finally, I was taken to the MRI centre. Have you ever had an MRI? It is certainly an experience that you have to get your mind to control; otherwise, your instincts could take over and fill you full of dread, particularly if you have a tendency to be claustrophobic.

The first step was for me to have a cannula put in my vein so that they could inject radioactive dye into me during the process. So here I was with a nurse who I was sure would not be able to get the cannula in on the first attempt, as virtually no nurse had been able to so far.

I explained to the nurse that staff usually had trouble with my veins. As soon as she started "feeling for the vein," I knew she would not be successful. It seemed that every nurse who patted my arm looking for a suitable vein failed on the first attempt. I assumed this would be no different; somehow, she just seemed to lack the confidence that the phlebotomists had.

I was always apprehensive when I knew a cannula was about to be put into my arm, as the pain caused by the probing and trying again and again became a trauma in itself.

But maybe this time I was wrong. In went the needle and I said, "Great, you got it in first try! Well done!"

"Mmmm . . . not quite," she said. "I'll have to jiggle it around a bit."

Well, after a couple of minutes of jiggling, she gave up and pulled it out. Then she said, "Let's try your hand on the other arm; the vein looks good there."

This time she was successful . . . and I mean successful! The blood from the vein spurted out and ran down my hand, then down the side of the chair and left a puddle on the floor. The blood-thinning injections I was on had certainly worked! "Woops!" she said, but she generally seemed unconcerned. As I didn't have to clean up the blood, I wasn't all that concerned either. I was just relieved that the cannula was finally in my vein and I did not have to tolerate more prodding, probing, and pain.

At long last, I was ready to go into the MRI machine. The technicians offered me headphones to listen to music. Now that is a laugh! The noise of the machine is so loud that you would never hear any music. So I opted for earplugs. Even these seemed pretty useless; it was only the voice of the technicians that was diminished (or so it seemed). The technician does speak to you from time to time and asks you if you are okay.

My head was rested in a U-shaped stand, which is not all that uncomfortable. Then a headpiece was placed over my face and attached to the U-shaped base. This is made up of strips of heavy-duty, plastic-like material, and I could see through the gaps between the strips. They then placed a mirror section over that so that I could see outside of the tube I was about to be placed in. Finally, foam pieces were placed between my head and the contraption just to make sure that I did not move my head at all. My head was now ready for the MRI.

A cushion was placed under my knees and I was moved into the narrow tube. I really wonder how very large people could possibly fit into this space. Then begins the cacophony of screeches, thumps, crashes, and bangs!

At times, I could hear a "washing machine" of swishes and swashes, a ship's horn blast away—there were often two lots of noises happening at the same time. There were medium blipping noises together with loud screeches. At times, the entire bed I was lying on shook and vibrated, seemingly from the noise.

I was pleased to get a short respite from the noise as the machine stopped and I was pulled out for the nurse to inject the radioactive dye through my cannula. She informed me that the "radiation" would make my brain "light up like a candle" and help them to see even finer detail in the images. I was moved back inside the tube and the noise started all over again.

I had no idea what to expect from an MRI procedure. I had not discussed it with my doctor or previously read about it. In fact, I had not even heard other patients discuss what happens. I believe that when you are facing the unknown that might create discomfort or distress, the best way to cope is to relax and keep your mind busy thinking of other things.

I actually worked out how to do a whole training routine to teach Cooper a new trick. Finally, I became so relaxed that I nearly went to sleep.

Now that I had gone through the MRI madness, I was looking forward to going home.

I was worried about Pete and I was missing him and my dogs and Rags, my ragdoll cat. I knew that when I got home, I would not be resting as well as I was in the hospital, but I would be worrying less about how everyone was coping at home.

When facing a new procedure that might not be too pleasant, make your mind think of other things that are pleasant. You will be amazed at how good the mind is at moving your body and soul to a new level of acceptance and tolerance.

CHAPTER 9

Preparing for the Unknown

I was sent home by ambulance as Pete could not pick me up. As I was being taken to the ambulance, I was handed a disc of the MRI for me to look at in my own time.

After a one-hour drive, I arrived home and the ambulance officers assisted me inside after Pete struggled to the door to open it. My two little dogs were bouncing around and whining in excitement, as delighted to see me as I was to see them. Even Rags showed uncharacteristic affection, and I had all three of them on my knee as soon as I was seated in my easy chair.

I am sure my mother was pleased to see me. She did not make any fuss or ask any questions, but I did get a peck on the cheek. Mum did not appear too distracted by the thought of my impending operation. Even though Pete sat with her each night after visiting me and told her how I was doing, he had been careful not to give her too much detailed information that might upset her; he kept everything low key. The last thing we wanted was for her to be distressed, as she tended to have panic attacks when that happened.

I nearly felt as though it had all been a dream. I was back in my familiar surroundings with my family and pets. I still got the meals for everyone and actually felt quite normal—that is until I tried to read anything. If there were subtitles on the TV or just an ad with words, I would try to read them, but I could not. Being unable to read seemed to be the only real evidence I had that anything was drastically wrong.

I thought I was calm and accepting of the forthcoming surgery, but every now and then, I would get teary for no apparent reason. I was not actually thinking about what the outcome of my operation might be, so why was I teary?

Following the stroke, I would get cross with myself for dropping tears when I had so much to be thankful for. I was not paralysed; I could still talk and communicate pretty well; I could still think logically and clearly. The fact that I got tired easily, could not read, and struggled remembering specific words, names, and numbers seemed like minor concerns when I considered what might have been the outcome of my stroke.

But it was more difficult to think of anything associated with brain surgery, as I knew there was a multitude of potential problems that could occur. But really, it was up to my surgeon. Again, I had no control over what might happen, so I saw no sense in worrying about it.

Nevertheless, I decided to write a letter to all my close family just to remind them of some of the great memories we have and to tell them not to worry. I thought that if anything terrible did happen, then the last thing they would have received from me was something positive and loving. I was following my belief: "Expect the best will happen, but be prepared for the worst." Perhaps there was a tinge of doubt in my subconscious, but I was not actually aware of any obvious concern or tension.

Of course, I also wrote a letter to Pete, and when I returned to the hospital for surgery, I left it on the car seat for him to find later. After my operation, he told me that it was the sweetest thing he had ever received from me, and it helped him a great deal to keep a positive attitude while he waited for me during my surgery.

I wonder how many people who are facing a life-and-death operation consider writing such letters. I think it is a great idea when the letters focus on the wonderful memories and do not dwell on any possible problems. Writing made me remember these great times in my past and brought my mind closer to my loved ones, not because I might lose them but simply because I love them.

I actually had my sixty-seventh birthday while home that week. No visitors, gifts, or fanfare—in fact, it might not even have been my birthday. Mark, Mum, Pete, and I were just pleased to be with each other at home; that was my gift: to be together.

One of the things that seemed weird to me was that I could not remember how old I was, yet I knew the date of my birth. During that week I was home, I remember seeing an interview of a TV star who said something about being forty-seven years old. I said to Pete, "Gee, she carries her age well, considering she is my age."

Pete looked at me oddly and then said, "Barb, she is forty-seven. You are sixty-seven."

Well, at least I got the sevens right!

The day before my surgery, I asked Pete to shave my head. When in hospital with the stroke, I had seen the mess made of the hair of some of the patients who had had brain surgery. I did not want great chunks and clumps of hair cut by the hospital staff, which tended to just shave patches here and there. I figured that if my hair was completely shaved, it would all grow back evenly and end up the same length as it grew back. My hair was pretty short anyway, so it was not a tough decision for me to make.

The anaesthetist had explained to me that I had to have a "halo" device screwed into my skull to keep my head as still as possible during the surgery. Then I had to have a piece of skull drilled out behind the left ear so that Mr. Bala could access the section of the brain where the tumour was seated. Consequently, I assumed that my hair would be shaved in a number of places.

Pete and I had a good giggle as he shaved my head and the hair fell to the floor. I was surprised at how comfortable I felt with my naked skull. My mum was more concerned than I was. "Oh Barbara, you look terrible," she cried. But I figured that she would get used to it. Pete and I thought it was a real hoot, and it added a humorous moment to what was really a serious situation.

The night before surgery, we decided to have a look at the MRI disc that I had been given when I left the Medi Hotel. We both were dumfounded. There it was: a big, white mass showing from every angle of the imaging. How could such a mass be growing in my brain and creating pressure on the brainstem that literally controlled my life, without me being aware of it? There were absolutely no symptoms that I had experienced. It is scary to imagine what we might have in our bodies and not have any knowledge of.

Pete thought that it looked like a golf ball. I was surprised how evenly spherical it was. It seemed to be so deep inside the brain, and it was, as the brainstem is at the centre of the brain. I knew that seven centimetres was a long way for Mr. Bala to get into the brain without causing any damage. But I still was not scared. I guess I have faith in doctors and was not going to worry about something over which I had no control. I am not terribly religious, but I do believe in fate—what is going to happen, is going to happen. I would either survive this operation or I wouldn't. The odds were in my favour (so Mr. Bala had told me), so there was no sense in worrying. I might as well relax and believe that the outcome would be good. The alternative was to worry and fret and perhaps even hinder my recovery.

I slept well that night. There was no anxiety or stress. I was just thankful that Pete's back had improved enough for him to drive me to the hospital. All seemed well. I had no fear or premonition that anything bad would happen. I knew that I just had to give myself time to heal after surgery. That was my philosophy (think positive and be prepared), and it had proven to be helpful in the past, so why not now?

Take the time to write or record messages to your loved ones before you have to face major surgery. Don't dwell on the possible consequences, but rather concentrate on the wonderful, warm memories that you have. This is your opportunity to send them a love letter.

CHAPTER 10

Major Surgery and the Aftermath

I was told that I was the first on the theatre list for the day of my operation. I was surprised that I did not have to be at the hospital until the morning of the actual surgery. I thought I would have to go in the night before. I had to be at the hospital at 7.00 a.m., which meant that we had to get up at 4.00 a.m. to give us time to drive there and not get caught up in the peak-hour traffic.

As we drove from home to the hospital, Pete and I did not talk, but we seldom did while we were driving. I was not thinking of anything in particular; I was just watching the beautiful landscape slowly take on its persona as the sun crept up. That wintery day, I was spellbound by the beauty of the frost on the grass in the paddocks. It was just visible as the sky took on some light and the sun edged its way through the mist. The fog hung low in patches and blocked my vision of the cattle and trees. I wondered what the cattle thought when munching on their crisp, frosty grass.

When we arrived at the hospital, we had to enter via a special door in the emergency department, as the main doors were not open so early in the morning. I wore a woollen hat over my shaved head and Pete carried my small bag of essentials.

I have been asked if I was nervous or worried before surgery. I can honestly say I was not. It was just another incident I had to accept. I did not consider the possible consequences; after all, what was the sense in worrying about something that might not happen?

I went into that section of the hospital that prepared patients for surgery by having them change into those "fashionable gowns" that don't cover you properly. I had to answer questions for the nurse to add to my growing set of records, and all the time, Pete sat with me. I thought he looked more uptight than I felt.

Then I had to lie on a bed, which was wheeled to another area, with Pete closely following. I was left waiting—but not for long. Mr. Bala came to see me with two assisting surgeons and had a short chat. I can't remember exactly what was said, other than he commented on my shaved head. His head was also shaved and he asked, "Are you copying my hairstyle?"

"Of course," I replied. "We can't have only you with such a fashionable hairstyle." I then said, "I hope you had a good night's sleep so that you are fresh and energised!" He assured me that he had.

"It's time to go," one of the surgeons finally said.

Pete gave me a kiss and squeezed my hand. "See you soon, love," he said in a slightly choked voice.

"Sure thing," I replied, hoping that I sounded cheerful and positive. I did not want to worry Pete and wanted him to keep his spirits up.

I was then wheeled into a room that was just big enough for my bed, the anaesthetist, and a nurse. Again, I had to cope with the pain of the doctor trying to put a cannula in a vein through which drips were fed during surgery.

This time was not going to be any different. When the anaesthetist was about to try for the third time, he told the nurse to prepare a local anaesthetic so that I would not feel the pain of him trying to push the cannula in. I remember the sting of the needle with the local anaesthetic, but I don't remember anything else until I was in the recovery ward.

I was in recovery for two hours, which is longer than usual, but I could not stop being sick. Mr. Bala eventually explained to me why I was so sick. "Unfortunately, the part of the brain that was touched when trying to reach the tumour was the part that controls vomiting and nausea."

Subsequently, my being sick and feeling nauseous was prolonged and severe. For three days, I did not keep even a sip of water down. However, I did have a drip inserted to keep up my fluids.

My mouth was so dry that my lips were peeling. I rinsed my mouth with water when I could and Pete put cream on my lips. Every time I moved at all, I was sick. I was given a special bag with a circular opening to be sick into, but every time I used it, I missed.

It is probably hard to imagine, but my missing the bag became a real source of amusement for me. Even though I was not eating or drinking, I desperately wanted to clean my teeth, so Pete helped me. Sure enough, when I tried to spit the water into the bag, I missed and spurted right over the top. The next day, I decided not to spit so strongly and missed again; this time, it dribbled down my chin instead of into the bag. I just saw this as so terribly funny. Of all the things that could have gone wrong, my missing the bag seemed the worst. Eventually, my aim did improve.

Mr. Bala came to see me and gave me some good news. "The tumour was not malignant, and I was able to get it out cleanly. I really don't think it will grow back, but we will have to keep a constant check on it for the rest of your life."

Both Pete and I were delighted to hear this news.

"I told you it was nothing to worry about," I said to Pete as I noticed tears welling in his eyes. It was a great relief, and we could now concentrate on my recovery.

The team of surgeons kept checking my "smile" to see how much the side of my face had drooped. I don't ever remember having my face looked at or scrutinised so intensely by so many men before. The left side of my face had drooped a little, but as I did not have a mirror, I didn't get to see it. It did not take more than a couple of days for my face to be back to normal. My right side was not affected at all; I really could count my blessings. It seemed that the worst thing I was experiencing was the nausea, which I was told would disappear as I improved.

The other problem that I encountered was that I was totally deaf in my left ear. Even Mr. Bala said, "I didn't expect that." He warned me that it might be permanent if it was caused by a specific part of the brain being damaged. I would have to undergo some hearing tests to see just what the problem was and whether it could be helped with a hearing aid. This would take place when I was well enough to go to the audiology department.

While Pete sat with me and tried to make me more comfortable, he filled me in on what he had gone through while I was in surgery. He told me that he never felt as though I might die, but when I was in surgery for over seven hours, he began to worry about possible complications.

Pete's daughter Judy sat with him for five of those hours. As a highly trained nurse used to the major surgery of organ transplants, she was able to give him positive and reassuring support. She had to organise for her four children to be looked after while she stayed with her dad, but eventually she had to go to pick up the children. Just as she was about to leave, a nurse Judy knew very well walked by. They exchanged a quick hello and then both had to leave.

Half an hour later, Judy's friend came back and chatted with Pete for some time. Finally, Pete asked her if she could find out how I was going. She went and checked and Pete was relieved to hear that everything had gone well and they were just "closing up." and I would soon be in the recovery ward.

Make sure that prior to surgery, you and your loved ones have asked the medical team a bunch of questions. Have an idea of how long the operation is likely to take and what are the possible outcomes (both good and bad).

Be prepared as much as possible. Loved ones might have to sit in the waiting room for many hours and should consider taking a thermos, sandwiches, and fruit. It could be a long wait, and they need to keep up their energy.

CHAPTER 11

I Am "King Hit" in Hospital

I was in the high-dependency ward for four days. Day and night, there was always a nurse present in the room. They have a small desk set up so that if they were not tending a patient they could catch up on their paperwork. I did not have a bell to ring if I needed a nurse; I just had to speak or groan and one was beside me. It certainly made me feel happier to know that someone was there for me all the time, as I don't think I would have been able to find and ring a bell if I needed someone.

The day following surgery, I was to have a scan to check for any brain swelling and to ensure that the level of fluid surrounding the brain was acceptable. I was surprised that I was not suffering much pain at all and later was told that the brain does not experience pain; it seemed as though my main problem was just vomiting and nausea. In hindsight, I think patients should be informed before brain surgery that the brain does not feel pain, as potential pain is something we all worry about.

An orderly arrived to take me, in my bed, to where I had to have the scan. He pushed my bed around until it was facing the door, and there he stopped while the nurse checked my wristband and my charts and handed the latter to the orderly to take with me. It was at this time that I noticed two women enter the room. One was an older lady, perhaps in her sixties and in a dressing gown, and a younger woman was perhaps her daughter. As they approached the foot of my bed, the daughter put her arms around her mother and said, "No, Mum, you are not allowed in here."

The mother gave her a shove and the daughter nearly fell, losing her balance as she staggered backwards. With that, the mother (now beside me) swung her arm backwards and with all her might, crashed her arm forward towards me. This was a typical "King Hit" that you would expect to see in a street brawl. Her hand struck my face with such force I thought she had broken my nose.

There was pandemonium. I cried out in pain. Nurses came running, an orderly grabbed the offender, and ice was brought to me to hold on my face. I could see that Pete was beside himself with concern for me. And then came the apologies. "She is now locked in her room," one nurse said. "Are you okay?" another nurse asked.

Finally, things calmed down and the orderly resumed his job of taking me to be scanned. In all the turmoil, I don't think the orderly moved or responded to the fiasco in any way. The whole situation was quite surreal.

Eventually, I had my scan, which showed that there was a fair bit of fluid around the brain, but there was nothing to worry about. Things could have been so much worse with such a solid thump to the head. For the next three days, I did suffer with a headache from the nose upwards into the front of my head.

Pete told me that when he arrived at the hospital that day, he saw the same disturbed woman attack a nurse. She attacked the same nurse later that day, bruised her face, and broke her glasses. The poor woman was suffering from a brain disorder and consequently had to be in the neurology ward (as I was) because she required the same group of specialists to look after her.

Later when my surgeon visited me, he was most concerned; but of course, he could do nothing. Thank God, there was no serious injury from the attack on me.

I wondered why they could not have made a blouse that had the sleeves sewn down the sides to elbow length, so that this woman's arms could not be raised high enough to carry out an attack on anyone.

"We are not allowed to use restraints," a nurse told me when I suggested this as a possible solution. However, later I was speaking to a lass who was studying to be a nurse, and in an exam, one of the questions asked was this: "Under what circumstances could restraints be used on a patient?" In short, the answer was, "If the patient is a danger to themselves or others." In this instance, I would have thought a restraint was necessary and acceptable, especially as I was told that I was not the first patient she had attacked.

It seemed unreasonable to me that both staff and patients were put at risk because another patient, with such a severe problem, had the right to freely move around the hospital and attack at random. She did have someone with her at all times, but it was obvious that that was ineffective and not a real solution.

I felt sorry for the woman and her daughter, but I was also sorry for myself, suffering pain that could have been a lot worse. It seemed that the hospital had its "hands tied" by not being able to take measures to safeguard everyone—patients and staff alike. I pondered over this for some days and tried to think of how I could make the public more aware of the problem and perhaps come up with a solution. There has to be a solution.

I did not know just how much this attack affected me emotionally until a day later, when a lady who was preparing to go home was standing at the foot of my bed and my attacker entered the room again. She put her arms out and moved towards the lady who was going home. I held my breath while waiting for an attack, but this time, she put her arms around her in a hug.

Three days after the attack, I was taken to a different room, as I no longer needed high-dependency care. Pete had been with me for some hours and was getting ready to go home when my curtains were suddenly pulled back, and there stood my attacker. She was looking at me. I panicked.

Someone came and took her out of the room, but I started to cry. "She has found me, Pete! She will attack me again!"

Pete tried to reassure me. "No, she hasn't found you, Barb. She doesn't know who you are. She just came in here by accident."

It didn't console me at all. I didn't care how she found me; the point was that she was not only in my room, but she had opened my curtain.

If I had wanted to escape, I would not have been able to because I was literally hooked up to my bed. Both of my legs had pressure fittings from the ankles to the knees. These were hooked to an electric device that caused them to pump, so that they kept the blood moving in my legs. There would be no way I could unhook myself and get away from the woman, if she wanted to attack me again. I knew I was being paranoid about this, but for the time being, it was how I felt and the danger was very real to me.

Eventually, the registrar came in to see me and said she would leave a note that the door to my room was to be left shut. At least my room had a door; some rooms only had a curtain. The door remained shut that night, but the next day with everyone coming and going, it was left open again.

The physiotherapist came to take me for a walk the following day, and as we were walking past the rooms, she asked if I was okay.

"As long as I don't have to go near the woman who attacked me, I will be fine," I replied.

The physiotherapist grabbed hold of my shoulders and quickly reversed me. Apparently, we were heading straight towards my attacker's room. From then on, all my walks were taken in the opposite direction, and I did not see the woman again.

Everyone knew what had happened and did their best to make me feel more relaxed and less threatened, but it took a couple of days before my level of stress reduced sufficiently for me to stop constantly looking over my shoulder.

Unfortunately, people cannot foresee that there might be such a patient at the hospital where they go, and all hospitals in Australia follow the same policy regarding restraints. There is always a chance of being a victim of attack by a fellow patient. Thank goodness, it does not happen very often.

If you are afraid or worried about anything while in hospital, ask to see the registrar. As staff members change shifts, your message to one might not get through to all. Make sure that your problem is sufficiently serious before asking for the registrar; after all, you do not want to be known as a whinger and consequently ignored.

CHAPTER 12

Caring for Others

I t only took a couple of days before I was well enough to be put in a wheelchair and taken for my hearing tests. One of the things they had to do was to put a tight band with an earphone over each ear. However, it was much too painful to put it over my ear where the surgery had taken place. This meant that the test could not be fully completed, but they were able to confirm that I had a considerable loss of hearing in that left ear.

The main discomfort I endured continued to be the constant feeling of nausea. I wondered if this terrible feeling would disappear, or was it to be with me forever? I had also lost my sense of taste. All food, and even water, tasted metallic. It was awful, and it took away my desire for food entirely.

"You must eat to build up your strength, so that you can get out of bed," a nurse said to me.

But I just could not stomach any food, especially the hospital food. Even their jelly tasted like chemicals. Pete tried to coax me to eat by making me a jelly with good-quality jelly crystals. He put it into tiny containers and brought them into hospital with nametags attached and put them in the fridge. When he visited, I would try to eat a couple of spoons of his jelly, but it was hard to pretend that I was enjoying it. Admittedly, it did not have the strong chemical taste, but it still tasted metallic.

The first few days after surgery my whole life revolved around nurses, doctors, and Pete. All nurses are kind and helpful, but a couple looking after me really stood out as having an outstanding, caring nature. They made me feel as though they were personally concerned about how I was coping and did everything possible to make me more comfortable. Of course, the surgeons were the same. But Mr. Bala and his associate, Chris, stood out in my mind as being exceptional. They would talk to me and answer any questions honestly and with kindness.

I got to know them quite well as they saw me every day and did not "come and go" as fellow patients did. I wanted to let both the special nurses and surgeons know how thankful I was for the way they looked after me, so I said to Pete on one of his visits, "Will you bring in half a dozen sets of cards that I have had printed with Cooper, Cameo, and Rag's images on them?"

"What for?" he asked me.

"I want to give a small thank-you gift to some of the nurses and surgeons," I responded.

So the next day, Pete brought me some of the cards. I have always liked giving gifts more than I like to receive them, so it gave me a great deal of pleasure to hand them out to my selected carers. They loved the cards and asked me about my pets, and of course, I enjoyed sharing some stories about how great they were and how I had trained them for the photo shoots for the cards. I was able to concentrate on something other than my illness, and I am sure giving these gifts went a long way towards building up my positive energy.

Even though I was suffering from the nausea and taste problems, and probably was not acting according to my normal behaviour pattern, I still tried very hard to be cooperative, understanding, and caring. A big part of my life has been dedicated to understanding and helping the underdog, but I do not suffer fools and unkindness lightly. I believe that we are meant to be kind and generous to our fellow man and that we have a responsibility to help those less fortunate than ourselves.

Once I had settled into the new ward and gradually improved, I became more aware of the other patients around me. It is always "pot luck" regarding the type of person you will be sharing your room with, and on the whole, my roommates were lovely people and struggling with their illnesses just as I was. But one patient stands out in my mind because of her unpleasant disposition.

She was about my age and suffering from multiple sclerosis. I understand that anyone suffering from this disease has to be going through both physical and emotional trauma, and I tried to excuse her behaviour because of this. She was paralysed from the waist down and had to be lifted by a hospital crane when the nurses needed to change the bed, etc. She was in hospital because the paralysis was moving to her arms. However, she did improve after a few days and was able to get into a wheelchair.

The staff and fellow patients were constantly bombarded with complaints from her. One day a nurse asked her, "Would you mind if some of the students came in and asked you questions about how your disease affects you and how you cope with it?"

"Definitely not," was her curt reply. "I am not a guinea pig, and your students can learn from someone else!" she snapped.

The really disturbing habit that affected me greatly was that she would interfere by adding her thoughts and comments to any conversations that patients would have with their doctors, nurses, or even visitors. We all found ourselves trying to communicate in whispers and sign language so that we had a bit of privacy.

On the other hand, when she had visitors, they were all loud and noisy; unfortunately, her voice was particularly loud and strident. One day I remember the noise went on and on and gave me a considerable headache. Later in the evening, when the visitors had left, I had my TV on with the sound box beside my one good ear. The curtains were drawn and there was a semblance of peace surrounding me. After a couple of minutes, I heard, "Barbara, will you please turn your TV down as I can't concentrate on my show?"

I must admit I was flabbergasted. The sound was so low, that I could barely hear it! So I turned my TV off and put my music on. This was before Pete got me the individual earplugs, as I could not put the headphones on because it was too painful to put them over my wound. Consequently, I had my good ear over the one speaker and the other speaker was tucked under my pillow. Again came the voice, "Can you turn your music down?"

I began to wonder if my hearing disability was such that I did have it louder than I thought it was and that the sounds were indeed disruptive.

"Is the volume of my speakers too loud? The patient next to me is complaining about it," I said to a nurse.

"The volume is quite low and should not disturb anyone. Unfortunately, you are beside a patient who likes to complain," she assured me.

It was obvious to me that the patient next to me was going to make my stay in hospital more unpleasant than it might have been. It was just something I had to accept.

The bed opposite me was empty for a short time, until an elderly lady was brought in. She suffered from dementia, and when sitting in her chair, she would pick up the phone (often it was upside down) and make an imaginary call. "Helen, are you there?" she would say. "Helen, come in. Where are you?"

This went on for some time, and finally I said, "Hello."

"Where have you been, Helen? I have been trying to reach you for ages," she said in desperation.

"I've been really busy," I replied.

"Well, I need to know what to do with this shipment that has come in."

"Just put it on the bed and I will pick it up shortly," I instructed.

"Okay," she replied as she put an imaginary parcel on the bed. "Now what do you want me to do?"

"Just have a rest," I suggested.

"You mean, do nothing?"

"You have been working hard," I said. "You deserve a rest."

"Yes, I have. That's a good idea. Okay, see you later."

With that, she hung up the phone and relaxed for a good hour. But again she started calling Helen, until the multiple-sclerosis patient said, "There is no Helen here. Don't be so silly. Be quiet and go to sleep."

I was infuriated. "Don't talk to her like that," I said.

"Why not?" was the aggressive response. "It's ridiculous what she is doing."

"Well, it makes her happy," I answered, "and it doesn't hurt anyone."

"Yeah, when she does it in the middle of the night and wakes us all up, you will think differently."

The elderly patient didn't do it during the night as she was given medication, and the next day she was taken to a rehabilitation centre.

I kept thinking of this dear soul. She received gorgeous flowers nearly every day, but no visitors. Nurses would tell her how beautiful the flowers were, and she would say, "Yes, they are. It's my birthday."

The first time she said this, I said, "Happy birthday, dear."

Then the nurse quietly said to me, "It really isn't her birthday. She just thinks it is because she is getting flowers."

I realised that when the elderly suffer like this, they revert to innocent childlike memories or only remember the special things in their lives. It is then that normal people steer away, as I guess it is embarrassing and they don't know what to talk about.

But why? When we have small children, we play "pretend" games with them and encourage them to fantasise with imaginary friends. Why can't we do that with dementia patients? Regardless of their age, they still need the love and interaction of family members. It satisfies a part of their brain that no longer functions as it once did.

We are so busy and, dare I say, selfish these days that we are not prepared to give back to our elderly the special attention that they need and they once gave us when we were children. They gave us all the love and guidance we needed to grow into mature people, so it is important for us to "pay it forward."

Or is it that we simply do not understand how to interact with those loved ones suffering from dementia? I know with my own mother, I want to react with her as I have always known her. She was the person who looked after me and set the rules and boundaries for me to follow; I looked up to her as the figurehead of the family.

Swapping roles was very difficult for me. Trying to treat her like the child in our relationship just did not sit well, and I found it hard to adjust. In fact, it was Pete who was more understanding and had more patience with her. Consequently, she often went to Pete rather than me when she wanted to ask a question or just tell a story. Was I feeling guilty?

I thank God that while in hospital, even when I was feeling a bit down and worried about my own problems, I could still feel concern and compassion for others and was willing to stand up for their rights. When I spend time thinking of others and working out how to show them kindness, then I am less likely to feel sorry for myself and more likely to heal and recover quickly.

When you constantly worry and panic about yourself and what you are going through, things are bound to get worse. There is nothing more stimulating and satisfying than helping others. Always think about what you can do to personally help others, rather than spending an enormous amount of time worrying about your own problems.

CHAPTER 13

Touching My Heart and Soul

E ven though I met a number of patients, I didn't really get to know them, as I was only in hospital for seven days. Many of the patients were there for an even shorter time, and patients tended to come and go quickly and without warning. Most of the time, I did not even get to know their names. Therefore, it surprised me just what strong memories these strangers instilled in me. It seemed as though hospital became the focal point of my life at this time. It became my whole new world.

Sometimes, fellow patients brought a strong response from me, and at other times, they touched my heart, but at all times they affected my recovery in one way or another. They often triggered memories from my own past, and in that way, they became part of my personal life.

Around five days after surgery, one of the nurses commented, "It's great working in a ward of younger women; most of our patients are elderly."

All of us in the room started to laugh as we were all over fifty years of age and I was the eldest at sixty-seven. When we told the nurse, she was amazed. She said, "I wouldn't have believed that. I thought you were all under fifty years old."

It was nice to know that even after our brain surgery and the traumas we had experienced, we not only looked young but we acted young as well.

I realised how lucky I was that I could feel as positive as I did when I met some of the other patients. One lady (she was the youngest at fifty years of age) always had her curtain drawn. Her mother and two young men (who I later discovered were her sons) came to see her regularly. Then there was an older man who wore a hat and had a cheeky grin. He would visit her later in the evening when the other visitors had gone home.

She had bleeding in the brain, and the doctors did not know why. She was waiting for an MRI and was fretting because of being away from her work, as she had so much to do. Every time a doctor came by, she would ask if she could go home, because she had such a workload. I thought this was her main concern, but one night I heard her crying.

A friend had sent me a lovely little crystal angel to look after me while I was in hospital. I asked a nurse to loan it to her for the night and tell her that the angel would look after her while she slept. She accepted it and the next morning opened the curtains to talk to me.

Her story touched my heart and brought back memories. She was a single parent as she had left her husband because he was abusing her. She had been on her own for some years before she met a great guy, and they got along just fine. But her mother did not like him. One night, when her mother and her sons were visiting, her friend came in to visit as well.

After a few minutes, her mother said in an exasperated voice, "Visiting hours are for the family and there are too many people in here."

So the guy went, and that was why he started visiting her after hours.

I couldn't help myself. I just had to advise her to stand up to her mum and tell her to back off. Mothers think they are protecting or supporting their daughters when sometimes they are just plain interfering.

I told her the story of my mum, who had lived with me for twenty-eight years. I hoped it would give her the strength and determination to make a stand with her mum. I encouraged her to point out that a man, who was new in her life and still wanted to visit and be with her when she was faced with a possible serious health problem, was a man of worth. Many husbands leave a wife if she or her children have major health issues; yet this relative stranger was standing by her and comforting her.

The purpose of my story was to demonstrate to her how speaking up for what you believed in could have a positive outcome. Mum had been visiting me for my fortieth birthday and to watch my eight-year-old son, Billy, perform in a ballet competition. He won and was the Victorian solo ballet champion for that year.

The next day, I received a phone call at 4.00 a.m. from the police in Port Macquarie. They told me that my father had committed suicide and had shot and killed a lady who worked for him when she tried to stop him. He was being declared bankrupt and could not see how to cope without his business. It was because of this ghastly and traumatic event that I devoted the rest of my life to helping other people in business, trying to show them ways to succeed and cope with the stresses that occur in business.

My mum has lived with me since then. We got along fairly well, but Mum is a very critical person and consequently seemed to always think that other people were also critical of her.

In my home, she had the large rumpus room where she had her bed, a lounge, a TV, etc. and was quite comfortable. One day I was out, and when I came home, I noticed that she had moved some of her furniture around. I thought she had done a good job, especially as the furniture was heavy. I told her what a good job she had done, and she snapped, "You are always criticising me. It doesn't matter what I do."

I was speechless and went to my room in tears. I just didn't understand how she could be so aggressive towards me when all I had said was what a good job she had done! Somehow, she thought that I was just being sarcastic and was actually criticising her.

Pete had only been with me a few months, and he naturally came to comfort me and ask what had happened. I told him and he went to my mum and told her not to speak to me in that tone in future. Mum came straight to me and demanded to know what I was carrying on about. For the first time in my life, I screamed at her, crying and telling her that it did not matter what I did because it was not good enough for her. I was beside myself and quite hysterical.

Things finally calmed down and I realised what I had done. I told Pete that we both had to apologise, as we had not respected her as we should have. Pete did not initially think he should say he was sorry for something he believed he needed to say. But I convinced him that we had to live in harmony and that we had to respect her, as she was older and had lost her husband in an awful way. So we both did apologise, but Mum didn't accept our apology. For the next week, Mum did not speak to us or join us for meals.

At the end of that week, it was her birthday and I had bought her a gift certificate to have a facial and hair treatment. When I saw her that morning, I said, "Happy birthday, Mum," as I handed her the certificate.

She ignored the gift and snapped back, "What's bloody happy about it?"

That was it. With tears welling in my eyes, I responded, "Mum, if you are not happy here, I will help you move to Jimmy's house in Brisbane. Or if you want to get a flat here in Melbourne, I will help you find one and help you move."

I was so upset that I could barely get the words out amongst the tears. I somehow managed to continue. "You are welcome to stay here, *but* I will not have you make my life miserable. My first husband did that, and I divorced him. I have been happy for eight years since then, and I intend to remain happy." It was painful to continue, but I made a final point. "I will not let you make me miserable, so just tell me if you want to move and I will help you."

Mum never said a word. We both simply left the room and went our separate ways.

That night, Mum joined us for dinner and was her normal chatty self. Nothing was ever mentioned again about the entire incident. Some years later, something came up about rules in the home and she said to Mark (in jest), "Do what your mother says. I do. I am afraid of her."

My roommate listened to my story and told me that she would say something to her mother, as she did not want her mother to destroy her life either. Then, as happened frequently in the hospital, I woke up in the morning and she was gone. She had been moved to the Medi Hotel, but the following day she came in to see me late at night. She told me that she had had a conversation with her mum and things had improved.

She was discharged from hospital the next day, and I did not see her again. But I think of her often and hope that she and her new man are happy and that her mother learned to like him as my mother now adores Pete.

I have always been interested in people and all too often experience similar emotions to them, as I attach my feelings to theirs. This comes from me sharing their suffering and pain or their happiness and joy. Consequently, I will not attend funerals, as I get so upset that people try to console me instead of concentrating on the close family members. Instead, I go to the home and prepare for those visiting after the funeral. In this way, I can still show my respect while caring and supporting the bereaved loved ones.

I am always amazed at how people cope with life and the problems they encounter. It was no different while in hospital. Even though I might have been suffering, it was what other people were coping with that emotionally drained me.

These days, both men and women share a room when in hospital. My mum, who was a nurse herself many, many years ago, commented that she found this sharing unbelievable. "That would never have happen when I was a nurse!" she said to me when I told her. But I must say that it did not bother me. One way you knew that you had a man in your ward was when the toilet seat was left up. Perhaps (like in coed schools, where I taught for around twenty years), people behave better when both genders are present.

I had so far been sharing a room with only women, when a man in his early forties joined us. He was tall and well built and had a shock of unruly dark hair, which had been shaved in one spot at the back of his head and covered with a dressing. He had a big booming voice when talking to his mum and his wife when they visited him the first day he was in my ward. The nurse came in and told him that his surgeon would be there shortly to discuss his operation.

Then the nurse said, "Perhaps we can go around to the lounge area so that it is a bit more private for you."

The lounge area had a door that closed, and my immediate thought was, "Bad news." They all went to the lounge and came back to the room about half an hour later.

The wife was crying as she said goodbye to him. Nothing was said by any of the patients in our room, but we all sensed that the news was not good. The next morning at around five o'clock, he began to make phone calls to relatives and workmates. I heard phrases like "bad news," "no hope," "It's the end, mate," and "They can't do anything," but I also heard, "I'll be okay," "I will fight this," and "I've had a good life." No one thought to complain about the loudness of his voice waking us all so early in the morning

Later that day, he told me his story. He had a brain tumour and when they opened him up, it was so bad they could do nothing so they just sewed him back up again. He had the same surgeon as I did and I was so thankful that Mr. Bala, who was both caring and gentle, was the one to tell him his terrible news.

He worked with the fire brigade and other organisations that helped people in crisis. His workmates were obviously distressed as they tried to "tough it out" during visits. He said he intended to take his family on a holiday and then was going to try radiation and chemotherapy to see if the tumour could be reduced at all, to give him some more time.

He told me that the year before, his wife had survived breast cancer. He had two young girls; the elder was only twelve and was intellectually challenged, having the understanding of a three-year-old. Naturally, he was worried about leaving them, as he had been told he would only have about a year to live. As he told me this, tears welled up in both of us. I am crying even as I write this, wondering how he and his family are coping, or if he is still with his family. His plight affected me greatly, yet I do not even know his name.

Two days before I left the hospital to return home, I was moved into the Medi Hotel again to make sure that I could look after myself by getting my own breakfast, making my bed, showering, dressing, etc. My bed was near the window this time, which gave me more natural light, and the space was somewhat larger too. Opposite me was a lovely young lady who had a beautiful, serene presence about her.

She was noticeable for the constant exercise that she was doing. She walked up and down the room using her legs in various ways. She would walk sideways, backwards, heel to toe forwards . . . She went on and on for ages. Then she would close her curtain and I could hear some sort of machine humming. This would take place for about an hour, and then she would start another set of exercises while lying on her bed.

One day she had some visitors: a woman with two small children. One child was crawling and the other was a sweet little girl aged around three or four. They all sat on the floor to talk and hug, and the little one crawled up to me a couple of times to grin a "hello."

While they were there, the speech therapist came to see me and proceeded to give me some testing, which included trying to read out loud a short sentence. Then the therapist read a paragraph to me and I had to tell her the meaning of what I had just heard.

While I was concentrating on the exercise, the little girl started blowing a whistle. After a few seconds, I found I could no longer concentrate and I was getting a headache, so I asked her to please stop blowing the whistle. She stopped immediately, and while I continued with my tests, the woman and children left.

After I completed the test and the therapist left, the patient came to me to apologise. Her voice and accent were as lovely and serene as I had imagined it would be. She was just such a gentle, sweet person; it was a joy just to hear her talk. We struck up a conversation. She told me that she was a highly trained professional woman who had come to Australia for work, as there was little chance of her getting work in her profession in her home country. I then found out that she had multiple sclerosis and was doing everything possible to keep her body moving and supple.

I could not help but compare her to the loud, difficult woman who had been beside me in the other ward. What a difference not only in demeanour but in her whole approach to life. I hoped, as the disease progressed, that this gentle lass would keep her positive attitude and not become aggressive and belligerent as her suffering increased.

Then she told me that the children who visited her were her daughters and the woman they were with was a social worker. Her story was a sad one. Her husband had been mentally abusing her and she was deeply concerned that the children, who could hear and see his behaviour, would be adversely affected by it. She decided to leave him. She had custody of the children, and then she got the disease. Now her husband was claiming custody because she would not be able to look after the children properly.

So the children were taken from her while the court decided what to do. She was so sad because she still feared that her children would be subjected to the husband's aggressive behaviour, yet she knew that her ability to look after them was fast slipping away.

On one hand, she hoped that she would be able to keep custody, and on the other hand, she knew that she was already struggling to look after them and this would only get worse with time. The sad reality was that the husband would probably end up with custody of the children, as she had no family in Australia who could help her.

Here was yet another patient who touched my heart and profoundly affected me. Yet again, I was reminded that so many people had worse problems than I had.

These people touched my life then left me. But one thing is for sure: it made me realise just how lucky I was. How could I possibly complain that I constantly got the letters p and b mixed up when writing, that I could not remember someone's name, or that I didn't walk in a straight line? My problems were so insignificant by comparison.

The strength of people when the "chips are down" will always amaze me and make me grateful for what I have.

> Open your heart and *feel* for others and their suffering. Don't be afraid to hold their hand, give them a hug, or simply listen to their story. Their story is more important than yours. Become a listener and show your kindness and empathy. Your thoughtful and sympathetic approach will not only help them with their healing process, it will also help you.

CHAPTER 14

A Tough Time

The problems I was facing took on a less significant role for me, as I became more worried about Pete than I did about myself.

I guess one of the things that helped me cope with my ordeal was the closeness of Pete and me and the wonderful support I had received from him, which helped eliminate any sense of fear about what might have happened to me. I did not feel devastated or worried about what might happen or miserable because of what had happened. I was able to accept everything as another passage in my life and one that would create new challenges and make me stronger through my ability to cope, no matter what. Much of this positivity came from the support I got from Pete.

I recognised how difficult all of this was for Pete, as I saw him literally collapsing in front of my eyes. I was distressed that my illness had caused this meltdown in Pete and that I was not in a position to be of much help to him.

Pete was not only putting on a brave front, but he was able to remain calm, gentle, and caring towards my mother. The worry he was experiencing made him look exhausted, and it became obvious to me that inside he was in turmoil. I might have had a brain tumour, but Pete was having a brain meltdown.

Pete told me that he was struggling to get out of bed before nine or ten in the morning and even then was waking up tired and troubled. His doctor told him it was caused by stress and if he was not careful he would fall back into depression. Things came to a head when his back went on him again and he could not come to the hospital to see me.

Not only did I miss Pete visiting me, but I was very concerned about him as he was in so much pain. If only Mum had gone into respite care for the time I was in hospital, Pete would not have had the extra burden of looking after another loved one who could not look after herself. There was no way that Pete would force her to go into a nursing home. As usual, he was being kind hearted and more concerned for my mum's happiness than his own well-being.

Suddenly, my problems took second place in my mind, as I now had to consider how we could cope with the two of us suffering ill health when I came home. But worrying was not going to help. We just had to cope, and as long as we were together, I believed that we would be able to manage the tough times ahead. We would just have to handle it one day at a time.

Mr. Bala initially told me to expect to be in hospital and rehabilitation for around three months, so mentally I was prepared for that. It was therefore quite a surprise and pretty amazing to hear that I could go home after only seven days in Monash.

Whereas I had to wait for around five hours for an ambulance to transfer me from Warragul to Monash hospital when I had the stroke, this time the ambulance arrived before I had even finished packing! The ambulance officers had to find a trolley to take everything I had accumulated, like my music player, flowers, food Pete had brought me that I had not eaten, bottled water, and a suitcase of my belongings; there was much too much for them to carry by hand. "Where on earth are we going to fit it all?" one asked the other.

However, with some juggling, they did find room for everything, and finally we were all packed and ready to go. As we left the building, it was drizzling rain and cold. I realised that I had missed the height of winter, which was disappointing, as I really enjoyed the tingling cold of this season. However, there were still some cold days left for me to enjoy. I find it much easier to keep warm in winter than to keep cool in summer.

There was another man being transported in the ambulance with me and I hoped that he didn't want to talk, as it was still difficult for me to concentrate on a conversation. He was tall (his feet hung over the end of the gurney), and thankfully he did not push for a conversation, probably because I only gave a short answer to any question and did not offer any comments.

As we were driving along, I again enjoyed looking out of the back window at the beautiful scenery, though this time it was daylight. I thought I saw my favourite trees, wattle, in full bloom. But I figured they could not be wattle as it was not the right time of the year. But I was wrong. It was indeed the wattle season. I had lost track of time during my hospital stays. Dates, months, and indeed anything that involved numbers were quite confusing for me. It now seemed that recognising time spans was another problem I had to work on.

During the drive home, I had two thoughts. I was looking forward to being greeted by my dogs again, and I wondered how Pete was coping with his back pain. I hadn't seen him for three days and missed him.

We were about thirty minutes from home when the ambulance stopped for petrol. My male companion wanted a "pit stop," and they had to get his gurney out of the ambulance and push it inside to the toilet. Boy, was it cold with the back door open! Eventually, we were on our way again. My home was the first stop; the gentleman was to go on further to Sale.

While in hospital, I was surprised to meet so many patients that came from Gippsland, the same area where I lived. One of the ladies, Mary (who had her back operated on), actually lived just around the corner from me, and many other patients came from Traralgon, Moe, and Sale. I wondered about this. Were there so many from this area suffering neurology problems, or did Monash mainly handle patients from Gippsland?

Finally, we reached my street and I had to convince the driver that, when he went down the steep drive to the house, there was plenty of room to turn the vehicle. He was in fact able to back up right to my front door. I began to feel a tingle of excitement. Home at last! When I had left my home seven days ago, I was facing the possibility that I might never return. But here I was. I was so looking forward to being with my loved ones and pets again and getting back into a routine that I chose to follow.

Prior to getting out of the ambulance, they unclipped my safety harness, which was a very strong three-point contraption. The top section had a heavy metal buckle and when unclipped was hung over the back of the gurney behind me. My gurney was taken out and then, as the woman officer assisting me went to reach forward from behind me, she caught the seat belt with her arm. It flipped through the air, with the heavy metal buckle landing with a thud on my forehead.

What else can happen to my head? I wondered as I yelped with the sudden pain. My head had been cut open, a woman had whacked me in the face, and now a metal buckle had "donged" me on the forehead! It reminded me of my younger brother, Jimmy. When he was a kid, he had so many accidents to his head that we ended up saying, "If it is his head that is hurt, he will be okay." Perhaps that would become my motto now.

Dogs, husband, and mother greeted me at the front door. I managed to make a wobbly progress through the entrance hall and the dining area into the TV room, where I went straight to my easy chair and plopped down. Pete helped to wrap me in a blanket and put the heater on. It was mid June and the coldness of winter was very noticeable, especially coming from the hospital, which was kept overly warm.

The dogs both landed on my lap. Mum managed to reach me to give me a kiss on the forehead. Pete—poor Pete—struggled to move, and after tucking the blanket around me, said, "Would you like a cup of tea or anything, love?"

"No, thanks, Pete. I'm okay," I replied.

As I appeared settled in my easy chair, Pete gave me a kiss on the top of my head and struggled back upstairs to his bed.

I was finally home, and I didn't want anything except to sit quietly and reflect how lucky I had been and how my life would now change.

The next three weeks proved to be really tough. I was not supposed to go upstairs, as I was still wobbly, so I rested and slept in my comfortable easy chair most of the time. I had very little strength and found it difficult to walk in a straight line. I would tend to veer off to one side. I used Mum's walking stick during this time to help steady me when moving around the house.

In hospital, the physiotherapist made sure that I could walk unaided, but when walking in a narrow space with a wall beside me, it was easier to keep a straight line than it was for me now when I had to walk across an open space. At the hospital, I also had to practise going up and down a set of three "pretend" stairs. At first, I would have to hold onto the rail, but eventually I could manage without hanging on. However, my doctor felt that the seventeen stairs I had at home created a risk and told me to stay downstairs until my strength returned and my balance improved.

Mum has a downstairs room with an en-suite, which has support rails for the shower and toilet. This proved to be a great help to me when I showered. However, by the third day home, things changed.

During those first three days, Pete was able to get downstairs to prepare meals for us all. Then his back got so bad that he literally could not move and for four days was unable to get out of bed. There was only me to get all our meals and help him get to the bathroom.

At first, I wondered how on earth I was going to manage. I had to work out how I could get food and drink to Pete upstairs without experiencing a relapse that could cause a setback to my own recovery.

Standing for the length of time needed to prepare the meals proved to be exhausting and I would have to sit and rest. When Mark was home between 8.00 p.m. and 9.00 p.m., he would take the dinner I had prepared upstairs to Pete and often sit with him while they both ate their meals. So that was one trip upstairs that I did not have to make.

The other meals I prepared for Pete consisted of a thermos of tea plus toast for breakfast, and then I made a sandwich for lunch with a piece of fruit and biscuits for his afternoon tea. I would then put everything in a carry bag and head for the stairs. Every third step I would stop and rest. It was not just the weakness and consequent tiredness of my legs that was the problem, but when my heartbeat got stronger from the exertion, my head pounded with pain. By stopping every third step, I was able to stop my blood pressure from rising and consequently reduced the pain.

I had taught the dogs never to go past us when we were going down the stairs in case they tripped us. But going up the stairs, they would bound past us on one side and wait for us at the top, tails wagging madly. But while I was struggling going up the stairs during this time, Cooper seemed to realise that I was in trouble and never once tried to go past me. When I stopped, he stopped. Slowly, we both made our way to the top.

When I reached Pete, I would have to lie down on the bed and rest. I was exhausted. Then I decided to shower while I was in our room. I could not believe how weak I felt. I could not even squeeze the plastic bottle of face cream to get some cream out. I would have to hand it to Pete in bed and get him to squeeze some cream onto my hand. It was so strange to be so weak! All of this became a two-hour task, and by the time I went downstairs again, I was keen to get back into my easy chair and rest.

Even when Pete was able to get out of bed for a couple of hours at a time, he could not drive. I had our local council arrange for someone to do some housework and to drive me to the doctors each week.

I had been put on the blood thinner, Warfarin, and the doctors were having trouble getting the right dosage to ensure the coagulation factor was correct. Consequently, I had to have a blood test each week, and the dosage was changed nearly every time.

A couple of weeks after I had come home, I went to the doctors to have my usual blood test. It was one of the few days when I felt really lousy, but thankfully, Pete was a lot better and was once again able to drive me to the doctors. I was still suffering from the nausea and had a lot of pain, which I really had not suffered from previously. I was managing to walk with the aid of a walking stick in one hand and by holding onto Pete with the other.

The doctor called my name so I struggled up and began a slow walk towards his room. Suddenly, there was a tap on my shoulder and a lady bent forward. She said, "Hello, Barbara. How are you feeling?"

I must have looked somewhat vague as I was still finding it difficult to remember any names.

"I'm Mary and I was in hospital opposite you when I had my back operated on," she explained. I remembered her and what her problem was, but I could not remember her name.

We said a couple of words and then I went into the doctor's room.

My blood test showed that the coagulation factor was too low, and it meant that the dosage of Warfarin had to be increased. But this time, the doctor was worried. "I should increase your dosage of Warfarin, but that thins the blood even more, and with the pain you are in at the moment, and you really don't seem very well at all, I am worried that you may have a bleed in the brain. I think you should go back to Monash."

Pete didn't hesitate. We were on the road back to Monash hospital within the hour. It was a long and painful trip for both of us: me with the pain in my head and Pete with his back pain.

When we got to Monash, Pete let me out near the door of the emergency department, as due to building work taking place, he could not park. So I stood there in the freezing wind, hanging onto a post, while Pete parked the car. I could not walk inside by myself, as I was too unsteady on my feet.

Finally, Pete came and helped me inside where I sat for some time until I was taken into a room and had my blood pressure taken. They also checked my reflexes, eyes, etc. The doctor decided that I was not dangerously ill and sent me back to the waiting room. Eventually, it was my time to see a doctor, and I was taken to another room, where they decided to put a cannula in my arm for any IV treatments that might be needed.

This time, they got the cannula in on the third attempt and took the sample of blood they needed. But as they were trying to tape it down to stay there in case it was needed again, it slipped out. Thankfully they decided to leave it out for the time being.

I was then taken to another room and reflex tests started again. Doctors always ask the same set of questions—"What hospital are you in?" "What month is it?" "When is your birthday?"—to see how your brain is coping. They then asked me to squeeze their hands as tightly as I could and push my toes against their hands, both forwards and backwards. This was not always easy to do, because I had a sore toe with a nail partially lifting off and not because of poor reflexes or lack of strength.

Finally, a surgeon arrived from neurology. I recognised her as one of the team who used to visit me each day when I was in hospital and she recognised me too. Most of the staff did, as I was the only one with a completely shaved head. She sent me off for a scan, which thankfully showed there was nothing seriously wrong. I still had excess fluid around the brain and they thought that could be causing the pain. The good news was that the brainstem, which had been pushed out of alignment by the tumour, was moving back into place.

Thankfully by now, the pain in my head had subsided. The surgeon gave me two options. I could stay in hospital overnight and have the fluid drained via a lumbar puncture, or I could leave it as it was and the fluid would eventually dissipate. I chose the latter. I did not want to go through the pain of a lumbar puncture and my headache had nearly gone; so home we went.

Sadly, the long drive proved to be too much for Pete's back and he was again bedridden for nearly a week. It was a tough time for us all, but we managed by simply taking one day at a time.

There can be setbacks to your recovery. Don't let them depress you. Don't question why it is that you are suffering; keep in mind that many others are suffering even more than you are. Keep looking for that silver lining, and stay positive. Everything improves over time, so give yourself time to heal and to get over any setbacks that you might experience.

CHAPTER 15

I Needed Help

My friends all lived some distance from Drouin, and it could take them between one and two hours travelling time to visit me. Yet over the next few weeks, a number of friends did make the journey. Many brought food, which was good for Pete, but I still could not eat. I continued to manage on jelly, water, and a little bread and honey. Everything still tasted metallic and I just felt terrible when I tried to eat. But not eating meant that I was staying weak for a lot longer than I should have.

It was good to see my friends, even though it was still difficult for me to hold a conversation. So I would ask them a question about their family, business, or work and let them talk to me. Even with them doing most of the talking, when they did leave, I still felt very tired.

I was on two types of medication for the nausea. One was to help for the nausea caused by my lack of balance, and the other for the nausea caused by the brain surgery. It did not eliminate the queasiness, but I guess it did make the symptoms less debilitating.

Having to do so much around the house, so early after surgery, slowed down the progress of my recovery; I should have been resting much more.

Pete continued to suffer with his constant back pain, and I am sure my worrying about him also slowed down my recovery. Finally, Pete had a CT scan, and it showed that three discs were pushing on nerves and that he had arthritis in his back as well. So now we knew what was causing the excruciating pain, but there did not seem to be anything he could do other than take muscle relaxants and painkillers and have bed rest.

The next step for him was to see a specialist, and this was going to be a long wait, as we no longer had private health cover. We had had private cover all our lives, but then Pete was retrenched from his job and so was my son Mark (who lived with us and helped pay the mortgage). Our private health cover had to go as we struggled to save our house from being sold out from under us.

Pete was able to draw on most of his superannuation. However, like many others, he had lost a great chunk of it during the global financial crisis. We were in danger of not being able to pay the mortgage, but Mark saved the house for us.

Mark was a computer programmer and had worked with the same company for over twenty years. The company then decided to use labour in India to do a lot of their work and Mark was sent to India to train the staff there. Of course, what he was really doing was making his own position redundant. Finally, he was retrenched, but he did receive a good payment package, which paid our mortgage for that first tough year.

But there was no money for many other things that had been an important part of our lives, like private health cover. This meant that we had to join the public hospital waiting game. Consequently, Pete would now have to wait some months before he could even see a specialist.

Mentally, I continued to survive by coping with my life one day at a time. Giving minimal care to Mum and Pete and doing as little as possible in the home were all I could manage. While generally coping with this tenuous situation, there came a time when I desperately needed additional help.

Four months before my stroke, I had made an appointment to see a specialist at the Austin Hospital in Melbourne, about having my hip replaced. The other hip had been replaced eight years before and was a huge success, but now the second hip was causing pain. The appointment was made for the date, which was to be two weeks following my brain surgery.

When I had had the stroke, Pete rang the Austin to see if they thought I should reschedule the appointment. They warned him not to do this, as it could take up to twelve months to get another appointment. So I was about to make this long trip when I should have been resting at home.

The problem was that Pete was still unable to drive me. We tried to get a volunteer driver from the council pool, but there was no one available for that day. We were feeling desperate, as we did not know anyone locally that could drive me.

Finally, Pete rang his brother who lived in Frankston, a good hour's drive from our place, and then there was over an hour's drive to the hospital. The entire trip there and back would mean that there were over four hours of driving for him. Pete's brother is in his seventies and has had heart bypass surgery and several operations to put stents in his legs because of the narrowing of his arteries, as well as having had a hip replaced. Nevertheless, he agreed to take me, and both he and his wife made this trip to the hospital with me three times over the next few weeks.

These trips really did take their toll on me. They were long and tiresome, and together with my weakness and nausea, I easily became exhausted. I remember the day of the first trip well, as I was really feeling lousy. My brother-in-law got me into the back of the car with a pillow for my head. It was a difficult trip for me, as I was in pain and feeling so sick.

Finally, we arrived at the hospital and I have never seen so many people waiting for their appointments; there appeared to be hundreds. There was an announcement every fifteen minutes calling people who had appointments for that time slot. There were five different counters that patients could go to and goodness knows how many consulting rooms where the doctors would see them. I was in no condition to stand in the line, so my sister-in-law sat me down and stood in the line for me.

I could see her from where I was sitting and I thought there seemed to be something wrong, as she was in some discussion with the person behind the counter. Eventually, she came back to me and said, "Oh, dear . . . Barb, there is a problem. Your appointment has been cancelled."

I was dumfounded. Apparently the surgeon's wife had had a baby and he took a week off to be with her. I was devastated that they had not notified me. However, it turned out that they had sent me a letter, but it had gone to my post office box and, as neither of us could drive, we had not been able to get to the box. I actually thought that they would have made a phone call when changing an appointment. I felt terrible for my relatives who had gone to so much trouble for me, but they were wonderful. They found a wheelchair to get me back to the car, as by now I was feeling very weak and miserable.

Another appointment was made for two weeks later, and again my relatives had to take me, as Pete still could not drive. Before I had had the stroke, the hip surgeon had asked me to mail all relevant documentation to him. So I sent him the referral, the CT scan, X-rays, and the MRI scan.

When I saw the surgeon the second time, he examined me then went to his computer to see what documentation he already had. He had nothing! I couldn't believe it. After sending all that information, he did not have any of the test results. I was given yet another appointment for two weeks later.

Again my relatives took me to the hospital—at least by now they knew exactly where to go. This time, the specialist informed me that he did not think my hip was ready to be replaced and made another appointment for twelve months later. All of this was at a time when I should have been resting and recovering. It had all been so unnecessary.

There is no question in my mind that these three trips to the Austin actually delayed my recuperation by a few weeks. I felt that I really needed something special to take place to speed up my healing process. And finally it happened; my nausea and the metallic taste of food went away!

It was quite remarkable how quickly I improved after the nausea stopped. My appetite was back and I began to enjoy food once more. I began to feel stronger every day and was walking in a straight line more often than not. It felt good not to be constantly bumping into walls when I was walking.

Now that I was feeling better, I was keen to start work again. With some trepidation, I went to the computer. *Will I be able to use it?* I wondered. It did take some time to get used to everything; the first step was knowing how to turn it on and off. It was difficult to accept that I could forget such simple tasks. I had forgotten a lot of the basic processes, but I was able to gradually learn them again, with Pete patiently helping me. I think I cried more over my frustration to use the computer than I had at any other time during my illness and recovery.

As I previously mentioned, during this whole time, I really did not experience any fear or sense of dread and was not overcome with any form of depression. However, there was one occasion when I had pure hysterics, and perhaps that was the result of a build-up of emotions that I had kept under control for so long.

The leather recliner chair that I spent so much time in had a footrest section that, when in the raised position, did not leave a gap between it and the body of the chair, as Pete's did. This meant that I could keep the back of my legs warmer. The gap was also covered with leather. Consequently, it was impossible to see anything under the chair when I was sitting in it.

Cooper and Cameo were always around the chair to keep me company, and they loved to jump up with me and cuddle. It certainly squashes me in, but I don't mind, especially during wintertime when having them on my lap keeps me nice and warm.

A couple of weeks after returning home, as I went to get out of the chair, it felt as though I had caught my rug in it, as the footrest did not close smoothly. As I looked down, sure enough the rug was caught a little, so I pulled it out and pushed the footrest down completely.

I was going to the kitchen to get my breakfast when I heard blood-curdling screams coming from Cameo. She has a history of bad back problems and my first thought was that Cooper had jumped on her in play and hurt her back.

I went as fast as I could into the TV room again where my chair was and was surprised that I could not see Cameo—but I could still hear her screams.

"Where are you?" I cried desperately. Cameo was going deaf, so I really did not expect her to respond. I then followed the scream, and it sounded like it came from under my chair, but how was that possible? The chair was very low to the floor, with only a couple of centimetres of space, and Cameo is quite a lot bigger than that.

I got down on my hands and knees with some difficulty to look under the chair, and my mind could not grasp what I saw. Cameo was there and appeared to be without a head! I could see her body right under the middle of the chair, but there was no head visible. Her tormented screams continued. I was horrified!

I struggled to my feet, much faster than I had managed since the surgery. I thought that I would have to lift the footrest again, as that also made the seat of the chair slide forwards and up. I tried to lift the latch that would make the footrest move, but I couldn't get it to work as it was designed to be opened when you were sitting in the chair, not coming at it from the front. I knew I would have to sit in the chair to open it, but would my weight make it worse for Cameo? Once the footrest was up, I would have to get off the chair, which would be very difficult to do, as my legs were out in front of me and I couldn't bend them to help me stand.

I don't know how I managed to do this, but I did. I then went to the back of the chair to lift it up to let Cameo out, but as I did so, she screamed even louder. I was getting even more desperate and was bordering on hysteria. I figured I needed Pete to help me, but again he was bedridden with his back problem. What was I to do? The chair is very heavy and I knew that Cameo needed someone to support her weight at the same time as the chair was turned over.

I rushed towards the staircase to call Pete, but he was already at the top of the stairs. "What the hell is going on?" he shouted.

I was already heading back to Cameo and yelled, "Quick, Pete, I need your help. Cameo is caught under my chair."

While Pete was coming down the stairs as quickly as he could, I moved a coffee table away from the side of the chair, as I realised I would have to tip it onto its side. As I began to pull it towards me, I said to Pete, "Pick her up as I tip the chair. I don't know just where her head is."

I had only pulled the chair towards me for a short distance when Pete said, "It's okay, she's out and she is fine."

I guess it was the relief of knowing she was okay. I could actually see her and she was running in circles, tail wagging, letting us know that she was pleased to be out from under the chair and she did not appear to be hurt at all. I collapsed into Pete's chair and started sobbing hysterically. I had the shakes and could not stop. Pete had his arm around me and was trying to reassure me by saying, "It's okay. She is fine; everything is all right. Please, don't cry."

But I could not stop. I cried for half an hour. It seemed that the more I cried, the more I cried! Cooper was concerned about me and jumped up on the lounge, which was next to Pete's chair so that he could get across to me and nuzzle my ear to let me know he was there for me.

I am so very close to my dogs, as I know most people are, but Cooper was the first dog I had owned that actually *owned me.* He was very possessive of me and suffered from anxiety if

I was out of his sight. It therefore did not surprise me that he sensed that I was extremely distressed.

Eventually, I stopped crying and shaking, although I still felt traumatised. I thought I had killed my dog! I had nightmares about a headless dog for some time. I could not get over the fact that Cameo did not start screaming for about a minute after she had been stuck. I had a tradesman come out to check out the chair, and he showed me a circular hole formed from the metal supports. When the footrest closed, the hole actually closed to a very small aperture. Apparently, Cameo had squeezed herself under the chair and put her head into the hole to have a sniff around. None of us could believe that her head could be caught in this hole without choking her to death or breaking her neck.

This episode made me aware of how we are able to prioritise the degree of stress we feel. If something happens that is worse than what we are already experiencing, then our mind and body moves up a notch to help us cope. I think this is one of the reasons why I had mentally managed so well with my stroke and brain tumour. I kept thinking how much worse I could have been, so there was no need to be distressed over what was actually happening. In the overall picture, it was really not that bad at all.

To me, Cameo's plight was worse than mine, and once I had solved her problem, then I could let the emotional flow take over. Humans can cope so well with emergencies. We often hear stories of how people save others with what appears to be "superhuman" actions.

My family and I continued to cope "one day at a time." It was a matter of who needed the most help at any given moment. When I was feeling really poor, Pete was there to help me. He needed my help when I was barely able to give it, but I did my best. We were both thankful that Pete's brother and his wife were able to offer help when we both really needed it, and I am sure that Cameo was grateful that Pete and I were both able to help her too!

Don't call on others too often for help. Rather, only ask for it when you really do need it; remember the boy who cried wolf. On the other hand, don't think you have to manage everything yourself; learn to ask for help when it is really needed.

CHAPTER 16

On the Road to Recovery

As I continued to improve, it almost seemed as though my medical dilemma had not really happened. I began to *feel* normal. There was no pain from the surgery, but there was a sense of numbness on the left side of my head and often I experienced a tingling in that area, like a mild case of pins and needles. My hair was growing back and I began to look the much the same as I had before the stroke. Everything seemed the same: my hip problem; my mum's complaints; Mark still arguing with me; the dogs still loving me; and Pete remaining the ever thoughtful, loving, and caring husband who had his own medical problems to cope with. Everything seemed the same as it had been before the stroke; nothing appeared to have really changed.

Mark was going to work again, so I didn't see much of him, as he was up at 4.00 a.m. and did not get home until around 8.00 p.m. His first day at the new job was the day of my surgery, so he was not available to help until the weekend. I started to cook again, I painted some scarves for orders, and Pete and I began to revamp our main home based business website. We also undertook some online training to increase our skills. There is nothing like learning new skills to activate your brain and make you feel as though you are accomplishing something special.

Our life was slowly getting back on track. I sometimes wondered, *Has this serious medical condition really happened?* Yes, it had, and I was reminded of it every time I tried to read and could not work out a word or I literally "lost the plot" as I could not follow the storyline. Reading remained a slow and difficult process for me, but I persevered. I felt it was essential for me to be able to read again, and by constantly trying to read, my skills gradually improved from only being able to read that single word ("the") on the day after the stroke to being able to slowly work out words, sentences, and then paragraphs. But I wonder if I will ever be able to read a novel again or "speed-read" as I used to.

I remember sitting in the doctor's office while waiting for a blood test for the Warfarin about a month after returning home, when I noticed a sign near the counter. I looked at it for a while and then said to Pete, "Why would the doctor's office be giving away free margarine?"

Pete looked at the sign and pointed out that it actually read, "Free Magazines!" We had a good laugh. It has always been important to me that I can laugh at myself. A zany sense of humour was what drew Pete and me together in the first place. We love to laugh!

My brain would see some letters, and I would constantly jump to a conclusion as to what the word was—I was often wrong. I would then have to spend more time checking out the individual letters of each word. Most problems occurred with groups of letters that sounded different, such as ch, th, and sh. I also often confused a b with a p or k with a g.

The weirdest thing when typing numbers was that I often typed letters instead. It all made for slow reading, and often I would lose the train of thought as I read, because it took so long to get through three or four sentences; I would then have forgotten what the first sentence said. I would have to go back to the beginning and try again. To read a full page of text remains a difficult and sometimes impossible task.

Can you imagine how I felt about this? I was a teacher and an author; I had always communicated with the written word; not to be able to do so was so hard for me to accept.

Until my stroke, I had not realised just how much we let our minds skim across a number of words ahead of what we are actually reading. As I tried to read one word at a time, my brain would keep sending my eyes ahead. Then I would lose the entire meaning of what I was reading and all letters would become jumbled and seem like a foreign language yet again. I sometimes looked at a sentence and did not have a clue what it said. I had to keep reminding myself, "One word at a time."

I kept writing and practised reading every day in the hope that one day I would be back to normal. If that never happened, then I would simply have to be thankful for what I could still do and not fret about what I couldn't. It was that simple, and my reading problem was a small price to pay when compared to what might have been the outcome of a stroke or a brain tumour.

I still feel embarrassed when I get names confused or can't remember a specific word. When that happens, I seem to get anxious, and that just exacerbates the problem. It was certainly strange when I would say the wrong word or number and did not realise that I had done so. It was as though a word would just pop out without it necessarily being related to what I was talking about. If I said something and noticed a surprised look on the face of who I was talking to, I would stop and ask, "What did I say?" Then we would laugh and work out what I had really meant to say.

The hospital recommended that I go to a speech therapist to help me with my reading, and they organised an appointment for a local therapist in Warragul.

When I got there, I was greeted by a friendly young lady. "Tell me what you are currently able to do with your reading," she said.

"Well, I try to read my emails and my websites and blogs," I told her.

She hesitated and then said, "So everything you are doing in reading is on a computer screen?"

"Yes. Mostly it is," I replied.

"I think you should also try reading print, and I would have started you on children's books, as the sentence structure is simple and the words are usually pretty short," she explained. She then said, "But I think you would find children's books pretty boring as you are already trying to read business messages."

I agreed. I just don't think I could have coped with kids' books; it would have driven me crazy.

Basically, the therapist was in favour of what I was doing. At least I was managing to read subject matter that I wanted to read and therefore was more motivated to further improve my reading skills.

I was determined to read my emails and some of the newsletters I received. But often I could not read them in their entirety and Pete would have to read them to me. It must have been such a nuisance for him, but he never once complained.

Even when I was managing to read, it was slow and tiresome as I struggled from word to word. Complex sentences confused me. I seemed to panic and was less able to read anything at all when that happened. I would then have to leave the reading and do something else for a time before returning and trying once again.

Another problem I experienced, that did not seem to be improving, was remembering names, specific words, and numbers. If I gave myself time, then often the word or name would eventually come to me, but many times I had to ask Pete for help. Pete actually thought that my memory skills were getting worse. He thought perhaps this was because I was trying to move forward too quickly.

It was obvious that I could not do everything that I had been able to do and I realised that I would have to give up some of the activities that I was involved in prior to the stroke. One of the activities I decided to give away was as president of a business association that I had helped found eleven years earlier.

We called an AGM and I gave my first short speech to those members present. I struggled to give an account of what had happened to me, and as I progressed, my voice cracked and tears began welling in my eyes. Those present were understanding and sympathetic, and one kind member came to the front where I was standing and held my hand to give me courage.

As I planned to do presentations and tell my story to a number of groups once my book was published, I worried that I might not be able to give a professional account of my journey without my emotions taking over.

I had written my final president's report for the AGM but knew that I could not read it to the members, so I had asked our secretary to read it for me. She was delighted to do so. But when the time came, I asked another member to read. The secretary was somewhat flustered and said, "Oh, of course. Here is the report." She went to hand it over.

I then realised what I had done. I had mixed the names up. "No, no," I quickly said. "I meant the secretary will read it!"

As I closed this major part of my past life, I felt so sad. But I have always been able to cope with changes when I make the decision to do so. However, this seemed as though my illness had forced me to make the decision, and that was harder to accept.

The sadness I felt was soon followed by a happy incident. The day following the AGM, Pete was driving me to the doctor for my regular blood test when we drove past a group of houses only a couple of minutes from home. He pointed to one house and said, "That is where Mary and Bob live." Mary was the patient I had shared a ward with, the one who had back surgery and had said hello to me in the doctor's office.

A couple of weeks later, we were driving past Mary's house again when we saw her husband, Bob, doing some gardening. "Let's stop and say hello," I said.

We had a lovely chat for half an hour. Mary was also in the garden and had progressed well from her back surgery, although she still was having some numbness in her feet and was unable to stand for long. We invited Mary and Bob to join us for lunch at our favourite local restaurant. They came and we had a great time. This lovely couple, who we met during a time of trauma, became our friends.

Another hospital friend that I kept in touch with is Geoff. He always seemed so happy and full of life that I did not really think of him as being terribly ill. Pete and I visited him in his new home, which was a large, cold-looking place with no character or friendliness. It was clean and freshly painted, but it gave Pete and me the creeps.

"Do you like living here?" I asked Geoff.

"I didn't at first, but I've got used to it now," he replied.

We gave Geoff the watch we had planned to give him when we were still in hospital. I had baked some shortbread biscuits and also took them to him. He was very happy to see us and loved the watch and bickies. As he showed us around his new home, I kept thinking, *How can he live the rest of his life here?*

We finally sat in the lounge room, which had a large TV and a piano. No one else was there, except for a little bird that had flown in. Geoff tried to catch it, and after ten minutes, he finally did manage to grab it by its tail feathers. As he released it outside and it fluttered off, feathers flew in all directions. I just hope it was not too damaged and managed to survive Geoff's well-intentioned rescue.

Geoff loved horses and always wanted to go to the races, so Pete and I organised to take him to the local race meeting, which was coming up in three weeks. Two days before, we rang him to remind him, but unfortunately he was too ill to go. I felt quite sad, as this was something he really wanted to do. It also made me aware of just how ill Geoff really was.

My two new friends and I suffered differently, yet all three of us had to learn to cope and move forward to make our lives as fulfilling as possible. No doubt, it was going to be easier for some of us.

Recovery will happen over different time spans for all of us. Set up a chart where you can list the changes as they occur. It is important that you are able to assess your recovery step by step. Where possible, get involved in what you were doing before your medical condition. It soothes the soul to know that we can achieve a life that we enjoy and feel comfortable with. Accept that your life might be different in some ways and enjoy what you can now do.

CHAPTER 17

My Full Circle

After a serious illness resulting in hospitalisation, most patients are inundated with follow-up visits to doctors and therapists. There are many ongoing tests to contend with as well. We are never left alone for long and because of this constant and ongoing support, we are less likely to have signs and symptoms escape the attention of the medical team looking after us.

As I had made major progress with my initial recovery in hospital, I did not have to go to a rehabilitation hospital. But I did have to get myself to a number of specialists so that they could continue to assess and monitor my progress.

The hearing loss in my left ear was so pronounced. Once someone rang, so I lifted the phone to my ear and said, "Hello," but there was no answer so I hung up. A couple of minutes later, it rang again; again, I said, "Hello," and again there was no answer. Suddenly, I realised that I was holding the phone to my left ear, so I quickly swapped ears and found that I did indeed have someone on the line—I just could not hear through my deaf ear.

Finally, I got my hearing fully tested and was supplied with a hearing aid for the damaged ear. I was surprised at how comfortable it was to wear, though I did not feel as though my hearing was improved very much by wearing it. This was probably because the hearing problem quickly disappeared and it was a real relief when I could finally answer the phone to my left ear.

I also needed to have in-depth eye tests. They took place over two days, and I was surprised that the results were so positive. Since the surgery, my left eye had given me a lot of trouble with stinging and soreness and I was finding it difficult to see clearly out of it.

For two years, I have been showing early signs of macular degeneration, and I guess I will end up like my mum, who is now nearly blind from that disease. However, there is no use worrying about it, as there is no medical cure. I just want to produce as much painting and writing as I can, while I still have reasonable sight.

"After a stroke or a brain tumour, we often find that the eyes are adversely affected," the specialist told me. Getting good results from this test was really good news. Again, I could count my blessings.

Then I had to return to Monash for another MRI. This time, the noise was even more horrific, because my hearing had improved so much. After the MRI was completed, I had to wait a couple of hours before the surgeon looked at the results, and then he talked to me about them.

I recognised the surgeon as one I had seen while in hospital, and he recognised me too. He had a student with him, and immediately upon entering the room, he asked if I would describe to the student my inability to read yet be able to write.

I was anxious to know about the results of the MRI, but I did as the surgeon requested and told the student about how devastated I was when I realised I could not read but how delighted I was that I could still write. The surgeon I was now seeing had been with the group of surgeons who found me writing that first time and wondered if it made any sense.

The surgeon then told the student that I had alexia without agraphia. The student looked suitably bewildered at this unusual phenomenon I had experienced. The student had only read about it in textbooks before meeting me.

Finally, I was shown an image on the computer screen. I was looking at my actual MRI scan. I still had fluid around the brain, which continued to cause me some discomfort.

The surgeon was not overly worried, but instead of having me back for another MRI in two years, he wanted me back in six months to check the fluid again. I was told that if I experienced any other problems, I was to go back immediately.

Pete and I drove home relatively satisfied with my progress, but we were aware that we needed to carefully keep a look out for any symptoms that might indicate a further problem. I still had the feeling that everything was okay, and Pete said that he felt confident too. It was as if my confidence flowed across to him.

I guess the best way for me to measure my recovery was by comparing what I used to do with what I am currently able to do. I am still building my websites and making training videos. I am still writing books, blogs, forum posts, etc. I might be slower than before, and it is hard for me to follow a routine when I have so many trips to hospital, doctors, hearing specialists, etc. But on the whole, I am well aware that my recovery is nothing short of remarkable.

I see these medical follow-ups simply as distractions from what I really want to do. As long as I do not let them overwhelm me, then I will be fine.

It was important for my recovery that I remain productive and set goals for myself. I had a number of activities I wanted to get my teeth into, and this kept me determined and excited about my future.

I especially wanted to build on two of my websites that I had neglected. One is on silk painting, where I want to bring in other experts to share their knowledge and experiences with fellow artists. The other is to complete my Dog Training and Tricks website; it has been left unfinished for far too long.

Pete and I also intended to continue helping business operators to cope with the many problems they encounter when running a business. This was a commitment I made after my father's death, and I was determined to continue doing as much as I was physically able to do.

My silk painting business was also doing well. While I was in hospital, I had the largest number of online silk painting orders ever. Some were sending repeat orders as soon as they received the original ones. Fortunately, there were not so many orders that I could not manage, and it was comforting to know that I could still paint with the same high-quality results as before my illness. I was very worried at first, as I had the shakes and knew that I could not paint my type of intricate designs if I was shaking. However, this problem disappeared after only a few weeks.

I was "over the moon" when I was commissioned to paint a major silk wall hanging, about the size of a door, for an office foyer in a beautifully restored Heritage Listed building in East Melbourne. The house has been restored to perfection and is now being used as an audiology centre. The company wanted a colourful Australian design of birds and flowers to hang above the mantelpiece in the waiting room.

I made a series of videos showing my "work in progress" for my client. This not only allowed her to see just what was being accomplished, but it took away my worry of how long it was taking me to complete it, as the client could see just how complex the process was.

One of the five videos I made is listed on page one of YouTube and has had over 25,000 viewers. Completing this major project made me feel as though I was back to normal and had travelled the full circle.

My pledge now was to share what had happened to me with others suffering from serious illnesses and to hopefully inspire them to be positive. Once they could concentrate on what they could still do rather than on what they could no longer do, I knew that recovery was possible. This book was to become my first step in achieving this goal.

However, before I started to write this book, I wanted to know if my story would really be of interest to other readers. So I wrote seven posts, giving an abridged version of my story in an online forum, and I was overcome by the response. There were over forty comments left by readers, and over two thousand people read the posts. Everyone was so kind and caring. Best of all, I realised that my story did have some merit and was being seen as a story worth sharing with others. It gave me the added confidence that I needed to write this book.

Another business acquaintance and friend made a short video about the beginning of my story. This was to be used as a teaser to gain interest in my book and in inviting me to be a guest speaker. Before the taping, I practised in my mind just what I was to say. As I have always been good at visualising, this was not that hard to do, but still I was concerned that I would forget a word or lose my train of thought. However, I only forgot a word once. I was able to fill in with an alternative word, but it did make me feel rather anxious when it happened. This video was a huge success, as it made it to page one on YouTube and has had over 32,000 viewers.

Continuing with our work provides many challenges for both Pete and me, but I find them stimulating and can't wait to take the next step. I often wonder if this attitude is what has helped me overcome so many of my problems over the years.

I was also aware that I tire very easily and just cannot do as much in a single day as I used to. It was not that difficult to accept my slowing down, but it did make my daily schedule often seem somewhat outlandish, as I listed more goals than what was now physically possible for me to achieve.

What is normal varies from person to person. Normal for me was to *feel* productive, relaxed, and able to complete what I set out to do. This sense of normality wasn't the same as what it had been for me before the stroke. This time, it was based more on how I *felt* about what I could and could not do.

My confidence was growing every day as I improved in leaps and bounds. Any time that I felt I had not moved forward as fast as I wished, I compared what I was like when I first was in hospital with what I am like now. This is my reality check. My accomplishments in the specified time were really mind-boggling, and I constantly remind myself of how blessed I am.

It was so important for me to have the love and support of Pete while I continued my journey. By concentrating on what I could do, rather than fretting about what I could not do, I could set and reach my goals.

Of everything I wanted to do, it now seemed to be most important to be able to care for and help others in their hour of need. I now felt as though I had indeed completed my full circle.

Aim to be productive. Your goals will at first aim for simple outcomes, but will gradually progress as you stretch yourself to see what it is that you can now accomplish. You need to satisfy yourself and others. Reach for the stars. After all, you can do whatever you want to do; don't let anyone tell you that you can't do something.

AFTERWORD

This Book

Exactly twelve months to the day following the stroke, I signed an agreement with a publisher to have this book produced as a print book and as an e-book.

I was assigned a coordinator with a team of three to make the book look and sound as professional as possible. But the winning point for me was the fact that they put a great deal of effort into marketing and promoting the books of all their authors. In my home based business, I have always believed that marketing and promotion are the key elements for the success of any business.

As it turned out, it was more difficult for me to work through the suggestions for changes by the editor than to originally write the manuscript. Not being able to read the editor's comments or readily find the pages in my manuscript that the comments related to was an enormous challenge for both Pete and me.

It would have helped had the editor used the same numbers on the pages as I had in the original manuscript. But as the comments by the editor were in a column to the right of each page, the content on each page changed and the page numbering became obsolete. But we persevered, and this is the result. It has been an enormous learning curve for me, and I am so pleased that I was able to take it on.

My Health

It was weird. At exactly the same date that I was sent home from hospital between the stroke and the brain surgery, I ended up back in hospital—one year later! This time, there was concern that I might have had a heart attack. Thankfully, the tests were all negative, including the angiogram.

It was a relief to discover that my heart was okay as my racing heart, known as AF (atrial fibrillation), which I have had for over twenty years, was probably the cause of the stroke. Now when there is any suggestion of heart problems, there is real concern, as it could possibly lead to another stroke. I am pushing myself to do as much as possible to complete the goals that I have set for myself, just in case I find that further illness stops me in my tracks again.

The good news is that I am still not concerned and do not stress out or worry about something that I really do not have much control over and don't think will happen anyway.

Alexia without Agraphia

It was brought home to me yet again just how rare my condition is when Monash hospital asked if I would be willing to return to the hospital to take part in some testing they were running for surgeons who were doing their fellowship in neurology. Of course, I said, "Yes." How could I not agree? After all, they had saved my life!

Seven surgeons questioned me, within a fairly tight time span that they were given, and to my delight, all of them figured out that I had alexia without agraphia. It is good to know that in the future, these surgeons will know about this rare condition from firsthand experience rather than just having read about it in a textbook.

Peter

Pete still suffers with his back pain, which will probably never improve. He continues on his morphine patches and is now trying TENS (transcutaneous electrical nerve stimulation) to see if that can help at all. At the moment, he has had four days in a row without having to go to bed during the day. So we just hope for more and more days like these.

Unfortunately, he is now in a wheelchair because he has to have his knee replaced. He can barely walk, even with a walking stick.

Mum

Unfortunately, my mother's health continued to deteriorate. Her memory loss, caused by her dementia, got worse. She did not want to go into a home, even for respite care. However, I was not able to cope and my doctor urged me to get her into a home; otherwise, I ran the risk of not fully recovering from my own ordeal. It was not easy, but eventually I found a home in Traralgon, an hour's drive east of Drouin. Mum begged me to take her out of the home and it was a very emotionally draining time for all of us. But I stuck to my decision as I was struggling to look after both her and Pete.

Unfortunately, the second week she was in the home, she got a chest infection, and even though that seemed to clear up, she quickly went downhill and passed away within two months.

I will always feel guilty and will never know if being in the home is what caused her passing.

Celebration

I organised a luncheon at a local winery to celebrate my good health and my sixty-eighth birthday. Attending were around thirty friends who have been such great supporters over the last twelve months. It felt really good to have something so positive to celebrate. After all, when I had had my sixty-seventh birthday, I wondered if I would ever have another one.

I believe we should all celebrate as soon as possible after overcoming a serious illness or any other traumatic event in our lives. It is a similar situation with a funeral; instead of being sad for what we have lost, we need to celebrate what our loved ones were able to achieve in their lives. In fact, we should always celebrate and be thankful for what we have and put those things we feel we have lost at the bottom of our list.

Contact

If you wish to make contact to discuss your problems, or to ask me any questions, please feel free to do so. I am here to support you. You might also wish to view more information on my silk painting, Home Based Business Australia, or on my dogs.

Email: barbara@hbba.biz

Websites
www.HomeBasedBusinessAustralia.org
www.SilkPaintingByGabogrecan.com
Both have blogs.

YouTube Videos
My YouTube Channel shows fifty-one videos on a wide range of topics, including business, dogs, and silk painting: http://tinyurl.com/877x5ul.

Books

You can access information about the other books that I have written.

- *E-Book Marketing and Selling* (e-book):
  http://ebookmarketingandselling.com/
- *Business Solutions @ Work* (e-book):
  http://manual.solutionsatworknow.com/
- *How Do You Eat an Elephant?* (e-book):
  http://elephant.solutionsatworknow.com/
- *Are You Ready to Start a Business?* (e-book):
  http://startups.solutionsatworknow.com/
- *Fast Track Your Marketing* (e-book):
  http://fasttrack.solutionsatworknow.com/
- *Home Based Business Ideas* (e-book):
  http://yourhomebasedbusinessideas.com
- *How to Run a Business from Your Kitchen Table* (print):
  http://kitchentable.solutionsatworknow.com/

Have Your Say

In 50 words or less, send me an email telling me why you would recommend this book to others.

Each month a silk scarf will be given to the three most interesting and original responses received.

barbara@hbba.biz
